Object Oriencted Programming with C++

AUTHOR
Dr. PRATIK VANJARA

Object Oriencted Programming with C++

AUTHOR : **Dr. PRATIK VANJARA**

Inquiries should be addressed to

Dr.Pratik A Vanjara

c103,padmavati residency,

gautam nagar main road,

opp sterling hospital,gandhigram,Rajkot

Email: 369pratik@gmail.com

ISBN NO. : 978-93-84644-33-8

Copy: 100

Price: 175

First Edition (March-2015)

DEDICATED
TO

My Mother

A strong and gentle soul who taught me to trust in GOD,
Believe in hard work and that so much could be done with little

My Father

For being my first teacher

My wife

For earning honest living for us and for supporting and encouraging me to believe in myself

Preface

This book assumes you have n previous programming background. It used a step-by-step binding building approach to radiantly learn how to solve computer science and engineering problem in the C++ language.

Each chapter has three sections. Section A presents the basic theory and principle of the current topic. Section B illustrates these basic principles by using applications that are often found in computer science. Section C illustrates these basic principles by using application that may be found in the various engineering disciplines. You should study the basic theory section A and them study the appropriate application section of course anyone can benefit by also reviewing the other application area since they are frequently interrelated.

The book comes with the sample programs required for the programming assignments.

At the end of each chapter are **Design Exercises, Debug Exercises and Programming Problems.** Before you tracking any programming assignments, you should do both the Design and debug exercises. you will have a much better chance of success with drastically lower frustration level.

If you find any errors or have any suggestions or comments, please email me at 369pratik@gmail.com.

INDEX

UNIT – 1
Principles of Object Oriented Programming

que1.1: Procedure Oriented Programming :

⇒ The concept of Procedure Oriented Programming was introduced in 1960's.

⇒ Procedure Oriented programming basically consists of writing a list of instructions
(or actions) for the computer to follow & organizing these instructions into groups known as **functions** and always the primary focus is on function rather than data.

⇒ In the procedure-oriented approach, the problem is viewed as a sequence of things to be done such as reading, calculating and printing.

⇒ Generally we use a flow chart to organize these actions and represent the flow of control from one action to another.

⇒ And we all know that, when we are developing a function (procedure), we are having less concentration on the data, which is actually used by various functions. So in multi-function program, many important data items are placed as **global,** so that they may be accessed by all the functions and also each functions may have it's own local data.

⇒ **So the result is ....**

⇒ In a large program, it is very difficult to identify what data is used by which function. In case we need revise an external data structure, we also need to revise all the functions that access the data.

⇒ Another drawback is that the procedural approach does not model real world problems very well and this happens, because the functions are action-oriented not object oriented.

⇒ The technique of hierarchical decomposition has been used to specify the tasks to be completed for solving problem.

⇒ A typical program structure for procedural programming is shown in the given figure.

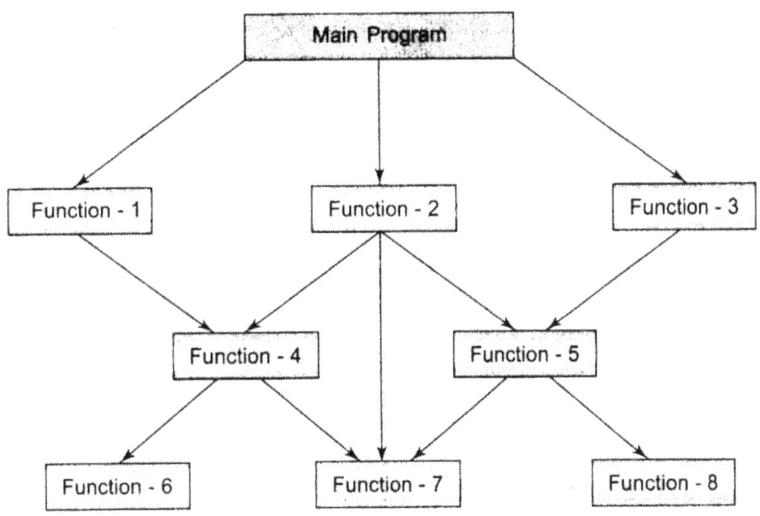

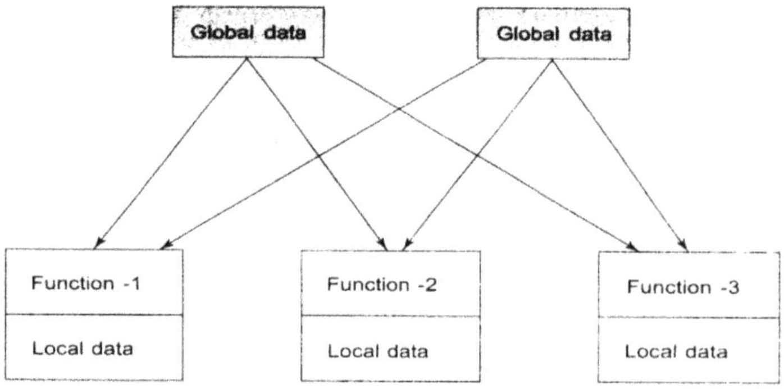

Relationship between Data and Functions in Procedure Oriented Programming

Some Characteristics of Procedure Oriented Programming:

⇒ Emphasis is on doing things (algorithms).
⇒ Large programs are divided into smaller programs known as functions.
⇒ Most of the functions share global data.
⇒ Data move openly around the system from function to function.
⇒ Functions transform data from one form to another.
⇒ Employs top-down approach in program design.

1.2 Object Oriented Programming:

⇒ Object oriented programming solves some of the problems just mentioned in contrast to the other techniques

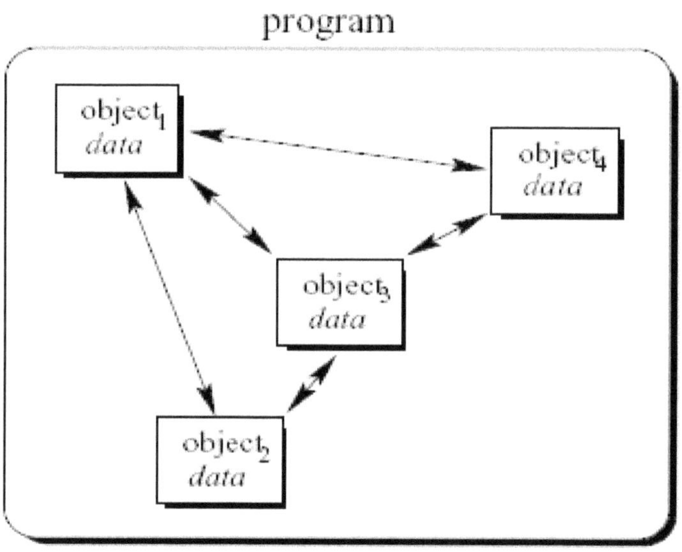

⇒ OOP is a method that allows the association of data structures with operations, similar to the way it appears in human mind.

⇒ OOP is an approach that provides a way of modularizing programs by creating partitioned memory area for both data and functions that can be used as a template for creating copies of such modules.

⇒ OOP treats data as critical elements in the program development and does not allow it to move freely around the system.

⇒ It ties data more closely to the functions that operate on it and protects it from accidental modification from outside functions.

⇒ OOP allows decomposition of a problem into a number of entities called objects. And then builds data and functions around these objects.

⇒ You can see the figure that shows how data relates to the objects? The data of an object can be accessed only by the functions associated with that object.

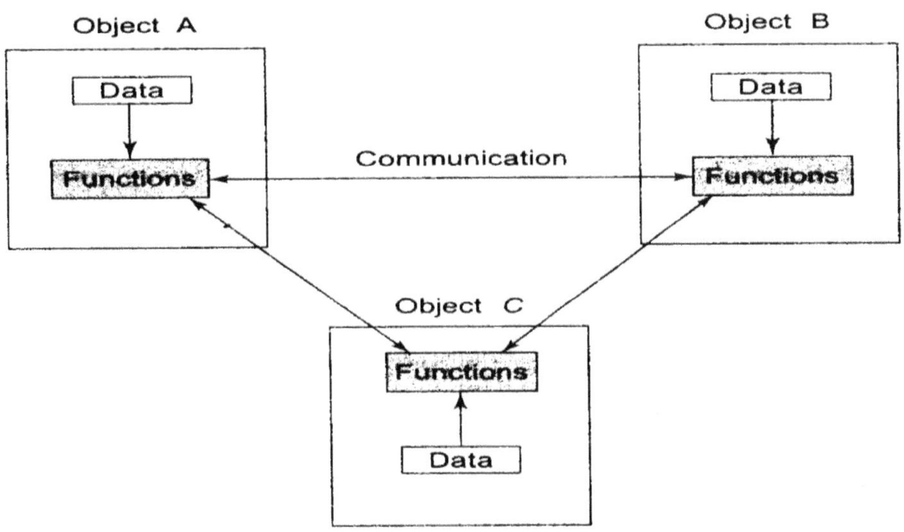

Features of Object Oriented Programming:

⇒ Emphasis is on data rather than procedure.

⇒ Programs are divided into what are known as objects.

⇒ Data structures are designed such that they characterize the objects.

⇒ Functions that operate on the data of an object are tied together in the data structure.

⇒ Data is hidden and cannot be accessed by external functions.

⇒ New data and functions can be easily added whenever necessary.

⇒ Follows Bottom-Up approach in the program design.

1.3 Basic concepts of Object Oriented Programming:

Object :

⇒ An object is an instance of a class. It can be uniquely identified by its name.

⇒ We refer to this possible sequence of state changes as the behavior of the object

⇒ Behaviour :The behavior of an object is defined by the set of methods which can be applied on it.

⇒ Objects are the basic run time entities in an object oriented system. They may represent a person, a place, a bank account, a table of data or any item that the program has to handle.

⇒ Program object such be chosen such that they match closely with the real-world objects.

⇒ Objects take up a space in a memory and have an associated address like a structure in a C

⇒ When a program is executed, the objects interact by sending message to one another.

⇒ **For Example ...**

- If "Customer" and "Account" are two objects in a program, Then the "Customer" Object may send a message to the account object requesting for the bank balance.

⇒ Each object contains data and code to manipulate that data.

⇒ Or simply you can say that, **"Objects are the variable of type class".**

⇒ Given figure shows two notations that are popularly used in object oriented analysis and design.

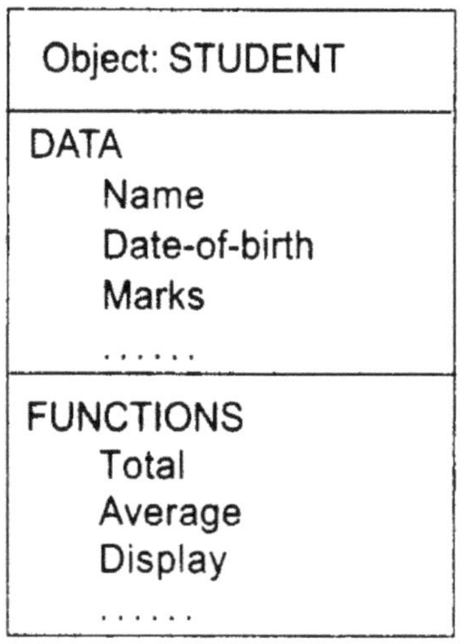

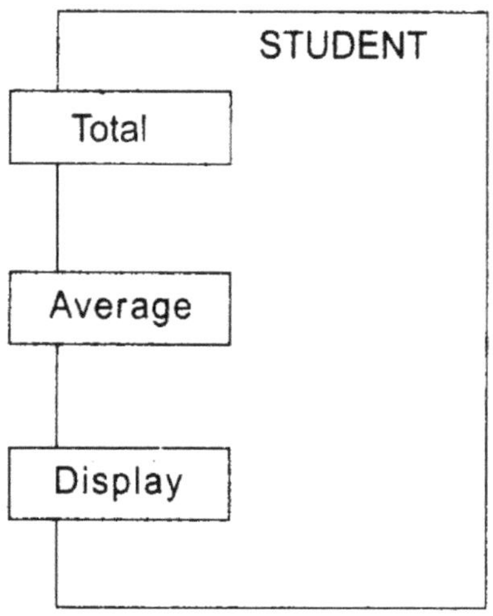

Classes:

⇒ The objects with the same data structure (attributes) and behavior (Operations) are grouped into a *Class.*

⇒ You can say that .... "A Class is a collection of the data and the code that manipulate the data".

⇒ Thus a Class is a collection of the objects of similar type.

⇒ Classes are the **User Defined Data Types** but behave like a **Built-In Data Type** in a programming language.

⇒ The syntax used to create an object is no different than the syntax used to create an integer object in C.

⇒ If fruit has been defined as a class, then the statement

fruit mango;

will create an object mango belonging to the class fruit.

⇒ The following points on classes can be noted :

- ***A class is a template that units data with similar properties.***
- ***A class is an abstraction of the real world entities with similar properties.***
- ***A class identifies a set of similar objects.***
- ***Ideally, the class is an implementation of abstract data type.***

Data Abstraction and Encapsulation

Data Abstraction

⇒ Abstraction refers to the act of representing essential features without including the background details of explanations.

⇒ Classes use the concept of the abstraction and are defined as a list of abstract attributes such as size, weight, and cost and functions to operate on these attributes. They encapsulate all the essential properties of the objects that are to be created. The attributes are sometimes called "Data members" because they hold information. The functions that operate on these data are sometimes called "Methods" or "Member Functions".

Encapsulation

⇒ The wrapping up of data and functions into a single unit (called classes) is known as Encapsulation. Data encapsulation is the most striking feature of a class.

⇒ The data is not accessible to the outside world, and only those functions which are wrapped in the class can access it.

⇒ These functions provide the interface between the object's data and the program.

⇒ This insulation of the data from direct access by the program is called "Data Hiding" or "Information Hiding".

Inheritance :

⇒ Inheritance is the process by which objects of one class obtain the properties of objects another class.

⇒ It supports the concept of "Hierarchical Classification". And also it provides the idea of "Reusability".

⇒ This means that we can add additional features to an existing class without modifying it. This is possible by deriving a new class from the existing one. The new class has the combined features of both the classes.

⇒ Note that each sub class defines only those features that are unique to it. Without the use of classification, each class would have to explicitly include all if its features.

⇒ The class from which the properties are acquire by another is known

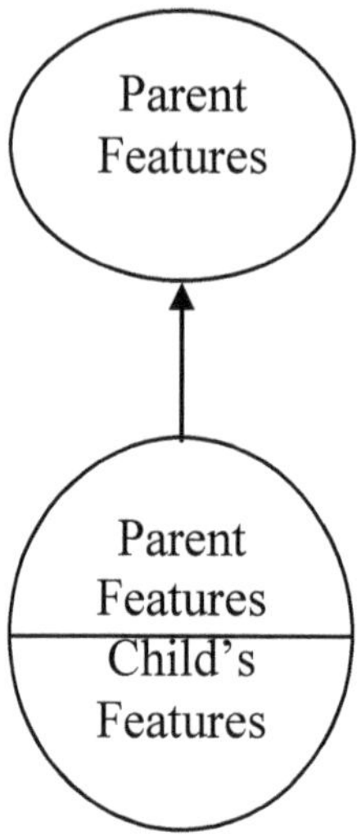

as "Base Class" and the class which gets the properties is know as "Derived class or child class".

Figure : concept of Inheritance

⇒ **Example :**

A house is a part of the general class called building. In turn, building is a part of the more general class of the objects that we call man-made. In each case, the child class inherits all those qualities associated with the parent and adds to them its own defining characteristics.

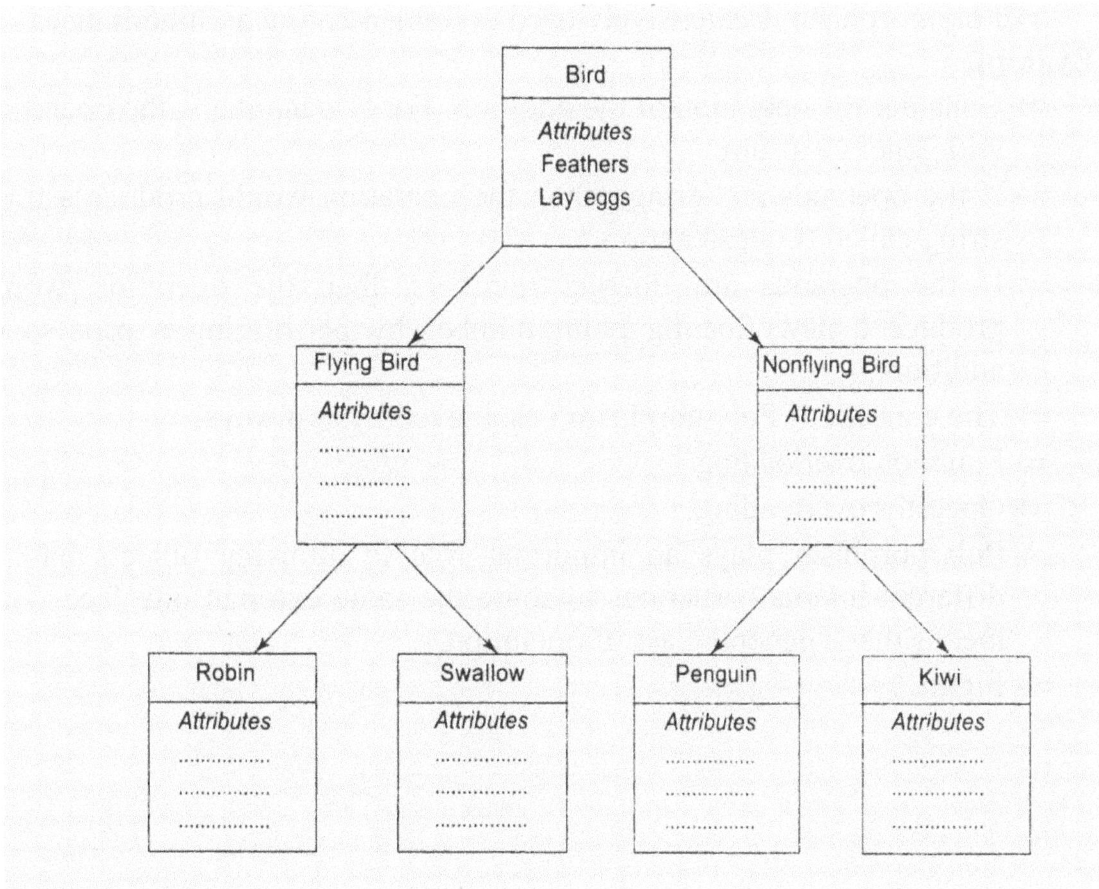

Polymorphism

⇒ The word Polymorphism is a Greek word, where Poly means "Many" and Morphism means "Forms" so the meaning is "Many Forms". Polymorphism is the quality that allows one name to be used for two or more related but technically different purposes.

⇒ As it relates to OOP, Polymorphism allows one name to specify a general class of actions, the specific action to be applied is determined by the type of data.

⇒ Polymorphism allows an entity for example (variable, function or object) to take a variety of representations.

⇒ The concept of polymorphism is characterized by the idea of "one interface, multiple methods", which means using a generic interface for a group of related activities.

⇒ The advantage of polymorphism is that it helps to reduce complexity by allowing one interface to specify a "general class of action". It is the compiler's job to select the specific action as it applies to each situation.

⇒ An operation may exhibit different behaviors in different instances. The behavior depends upon the types of data used in the operation may be accessed in the same manner even though specific actions associated with each operation may differ.

⇒ Polymorphism is extensively used in implementing an Inheritance.

Example :

⇒ Consider the operation of the addition. For two numbers, the operation will generate a sum.

⇒ If the operands are strings, then the operation would produce a third string called "concatenation".

⇒ If the operands are floating numbers, then the operation would produce a new floating point number by performing a process of addition.

⇒ The concept of Polymorphism is achieved by two ways.

⇒ Function overloading

⇒ Operator overloading

⇒ Polymorphism plays an important role in allowing objects having different internal structures to share the same external interface. This means that a general class of operation.

⇒ Figure :

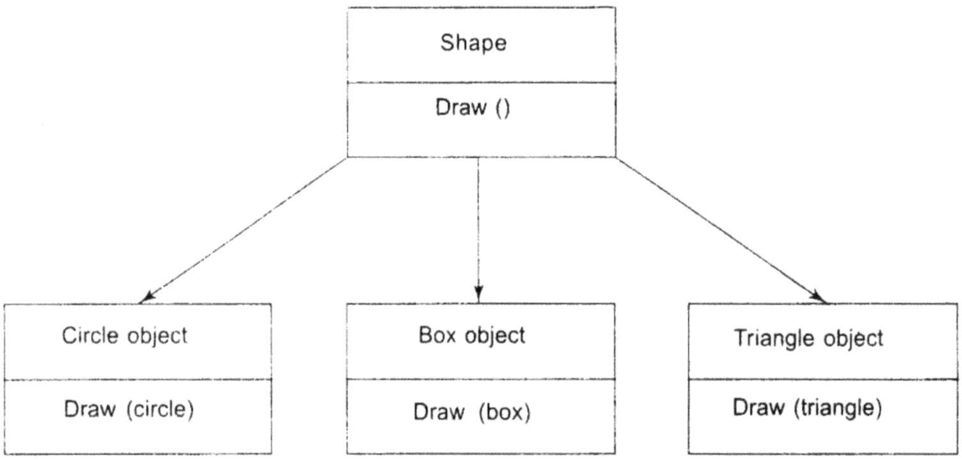

Dynamic Binding:

⇒ Binding refers to the linking of procedure call to the code to execute in response to the call.

⇒ Dynamic Binding also known as Late Binding means that the code associated with a given procedure call is not known until the time of the call at run time.

⇒ It associated with polymorphism and inheritance. A function call associated with a polymorphic reference depends on the dynamic type of the reference.

⇒ Consider the procedure draw () in the figure of Polymorphism. By Inheritance, every object will have this procedure. Its algorithm is however unique to each object and so the draw procedure will be redefined in each class that defines the object. At run time, the code matching the object under current reference will be called.

Message Passing

⇒ An object oriented program consists of a set of objects that communicate with each other. The process of programming in an object oriented language, therefore, involves the following basic steps :

1. **Creating classes that defines objects and their behavior.**
2. **Creating objects from class definitions, and**
3. **Establishing communication among objects.**

⇒ Objects communicate with one another by sending and receiving information much the same way as people pass message to one another. The concept of message passing makes it easier to talk about building systems that directly model or simulate their real world counterparts.

⇒ A message for an object is a request for execution of a procedure, and therefore will invoke a function (procedure) in the receiving object that generates the desired result. Message passing involves specifying the name of the object, the name of the function (message) and the information to be sent.

Example :

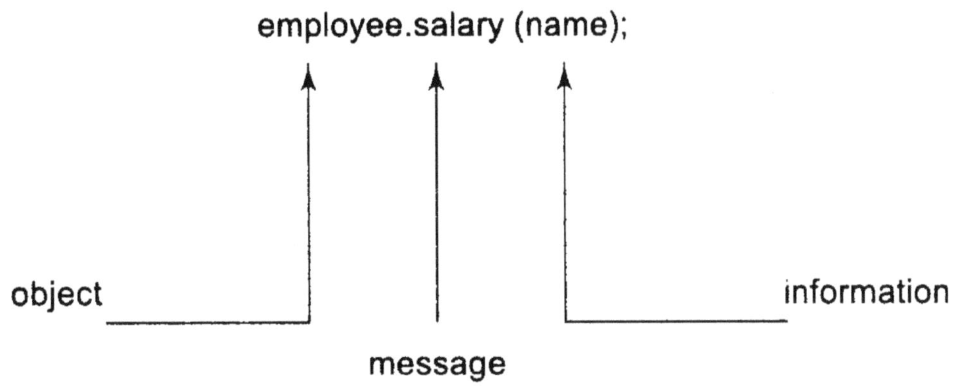

⇒ Objects have a life cycle. They can be created and destroyed. Communication with an object is feasible as long as it is alive.

1.4 Benefits of OOP:

OOP provides several benefits to the both program designer and the user of the program.

OOP supports several benefits. The principal advantages are as given below:

⇒ Through inheritance, we can eliminate redundant code and extend the use of existing classes.

⇒ We can build programs from the standard working modules that communicate with one another, rather than having to start writing the code from scratch. This leads to saving of development time and higher productivity.

⇒ The principle of data hiding helps the programmer to build secure programs that cannot be invaded by code in other parts of the program.

⇒ It is possible to map objects in the problem domain to those in the program.

⇒ It is easy to partition the work in a project based on objects.

⇒ The data-centered design approach enables us to capture more details of a model in implemental form.

⇒ Message passing techniques for communication between objects makes the inter face descriptions with external systems much simpler.

⇒ Software complexity can be easily managed.

1.5 Applications of OOP :

OOP Provides Many Applications :

⇒ **Real time Systems :**
A real time system is a system that give output at given instant and its parameters changes at every time. A real time system is nothing but a dynamic system. Dynamic means the system that changes every moment based on input to the system. OOP approach is very useful for Real time system because code changing is very easy in OOP system and it leads toward dynamic behaviour of OOP codes thus more suitable to real time system.

⇒ **Simulation and Modeling :**
System modeling is another area where criteria for OOP approach is countable. Representing a system is very easy in OOP approach because OOP codes are very easy to understand and thus is preferred to represent a system in simpler form.

⇒ **Hypertext and Hypermedia: -**
Hypertext and hypermedia is another area where OOP approach is spreading its legs. Its ease of using OOP codes that makes it suitable for various media approaches.

⇒ **Decision support system :**
Decision support system is an example of Real time system that too very advance and complex system. More details is explained in real time system.

⇒ **CAM/CAE/CAD System :**
Computer has wide use of OOP approach. This is due to time saving in writing OOP codes and dynamic behavior of OOP codes.

⇒ **Office Automation System :**
Automation system is just a part or type of real time system. Embeded systems make it easy to use OOP for automated system.

⇒ **AI and expert system :**
It is mixed system having both hypermedia and real time system.

que1.6 : What is C++ ?

⇒ C++ is an object oriented programming language.

⇒ It was developed by Bjarne Stroustrup at AT&T Bell Laboratory. In the early 1980's.

⇒ C++ is evolved from a talk of C that supports the object oriented features and still has the elegance and power of C.

⇒ There for C++ is an extension of C with major addition of Class, a construct from Simula67.

⇒ Since the class was the major addition to the original C language, so Stroustrup initially called the new language "C with Classes".

⇒ Several key ideas are borrowed from the Simula67 and ALGOL68 programming languages.

⇒ However, later in 1983, the name was changed to C++. The idea of C++ comes from the C increment operator ++, thereby suggesting that C++ is augmented (incremented) version of C.

⇒ C++ is the "Superset of C". Most of what we already know about C applies to C++ also. Therefore almost all C programs are also C++ program run under the C++ compiler.

Heritage of C++

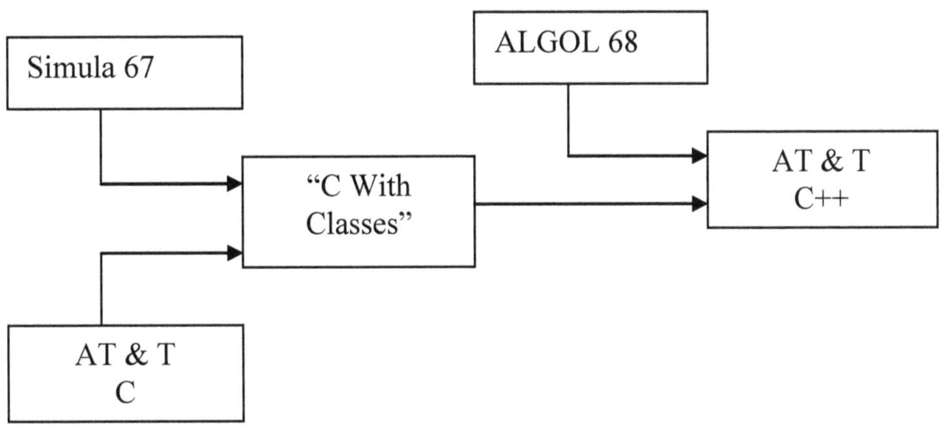

Why C++?

There are a few major advantages to using C++:

1) **C++ allows expression of abstract ideas**
C++ is a third generation language that allows a programmer to express their ideas at a high level as compared to assembly languages.
2) **C++ still allows a programmer to keep low-level control**
Even though C++ is a third generation language, it has some of the "feel" of an assembly language. It allows a programmer to get down

into the low-level workings and tune as necessary. C++ allows programmers strict control over memory management.

3) **C++ has national standards (ANSI)**
   C++ is a language with national standards. This is good for many reasons. Code written in C++ that conforms to the national standards can be easily integrated with preexisting code. Also, this allows programmers to reuse certain common libraries, so certain common functions do not need to be written more than once, and these functions behave the same anywhere they are used.
4) **C++ is reusable and object-oriented**
   C++ is an object-oriented language. This makes programming conceptually easier (once the object paradigm has been learned) and allows easy reuse of code, or parts of code through inheritance.
5) **C++ is widely used and taught**
   C++ is a very widely used programming language. Because of this, there are many tools available for C++ programming, and there is a broad base of programmers contributing to the C++ "community".

Basic Structure of C++ Program :

A typical C++ program would contain four sections as shown in given figure. These sections may be placed in separate code files and then compiled independently or jointly.

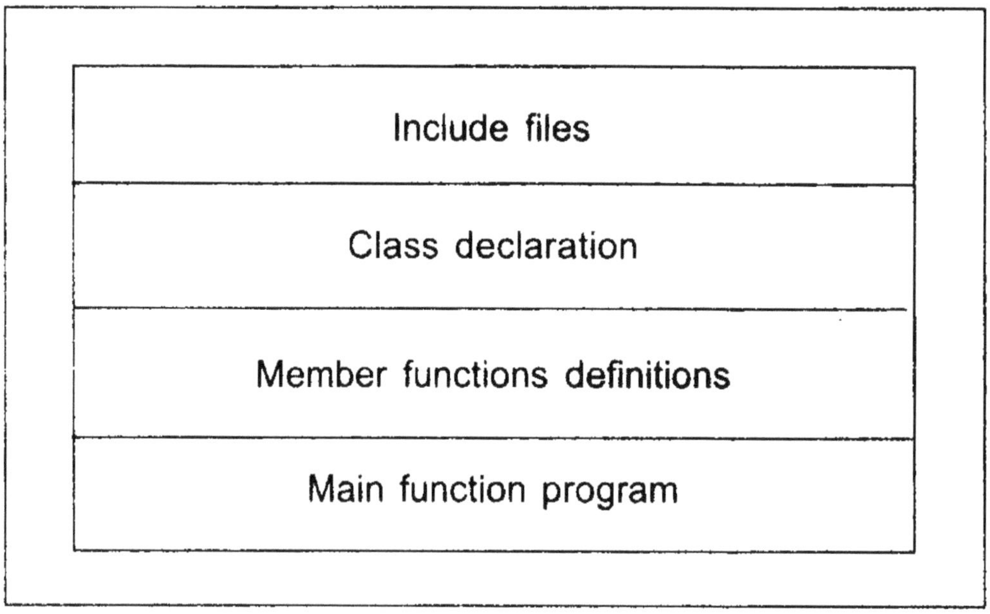

1) **Include Files :**
   ⇒ This section consist of header files whose extension is ".h" and consist of standard functions which are useful for build the programs. Functions like, cout, cin, getch(), clrscr() etc.

⇒ If you want to use cout & cin you must include the header file "iostream.h" and for using getch() and clrscr() you must include the header file "conio.h"

⇒ The header files can be including using "#include" pre-processor.

2) Class Declaration :

⇒ Class is a blue print of a system which is being developed.

⇒ In the program the "structure of class" is as given below:

```
Class <class name>
{
        ..........
        ..........      // body of the class
        ..........
}
```

3) Member Function Definitions :

⇒ You can define the member functions outside of the class also. So after declaration of method in the class, one can define the methods out side of the class also. As well as one can define inside the class also.

⇒ If you want to define the functions outside the class then you can do it with the help of the scope resolution operator.

4) Main Function Program :

⇒ However, C++ is an Object Oriented Programming Language but the execution of the program starts from the main method.

⇒ The main() function looks like this…

```
Int main()
{
        .........
        ......... // body of main()
        .........
}
```

Example :

```
#include <conio.h>
#include<iostream.h>
class student
{
        int age;
        public :void getage()
        {
        cout<<"Enter your Age :";
        cin>>age;
        }
        void putage()
        {
        cout<<"Your age is :"<<age;
```

```
        }
};

int main()
{
        student s;
        s.getage();
        s.putage()
}
```

The following points can be noted out from the above program.

⇒ The keyword "class" is used to indicate the class student.

⇒ The class contains age as a member variable.

⇒ It has two methods or member functions, getage() and putage().

⇒ In the main(), an object of class "student" is crated named "s", which will access the members of the class "student".

It is a common practice to organize a program into three separate files. The class declarations are placed in a header file and the definitions of member functions go into another file.

This approach enables the programmer to separate the abstract specification of the interface (class definition) from the implementation details (member functions definition).

Finally, the main program that uses the class is placed in a third file which "includes" the previous two files as well as any other files required.

Applications of C++ :

⇒ C++ is versatile language for handling very large programs. It is suitable for virtually any programming task including development of editors, compilers, databases, communication systems and any complex real-life application systems.

⇒ Since C++ allows us to create hierarchy-related objects, we can build special object-oriented libraries which can be used later by many programmers.

⇒ While C++ is able to map the real world problem properly, the C part of C++ gives the language the ability to get close to the machine-level details.

⇒ C++ programs are easily maintainable and expandable. When a new feature needs to be implemented, it is very easy to add to the existing structure of an object.

⇒ It is expected that C++ will replace C as a general-purpose language in the near future.

Input / output Operators :

The Input/Output operators are used to perform the basic input and output operations of the program in C++.

1) Input Operator:

⇒ The input stream allow to perform reading operation with input devices like keyboard, disk etc.

⇒ Input from the standard stream is performed using the "cin" object.

⇒ C++ uses the bit-wise right-shift operator to perform the console input operation. The syntax for standard input streams operation is as follows :

cin >> variable;

The word "cin" followed by a symbole ">>" (extraction or get from operator) and then with variable into which the input data is to be stored.

The object "cin" must be associated with at least one argument. Like scanf(), constant values cannot be sent as an argument to "cin" object.

">>" operator place the content of the input stream to the variable.

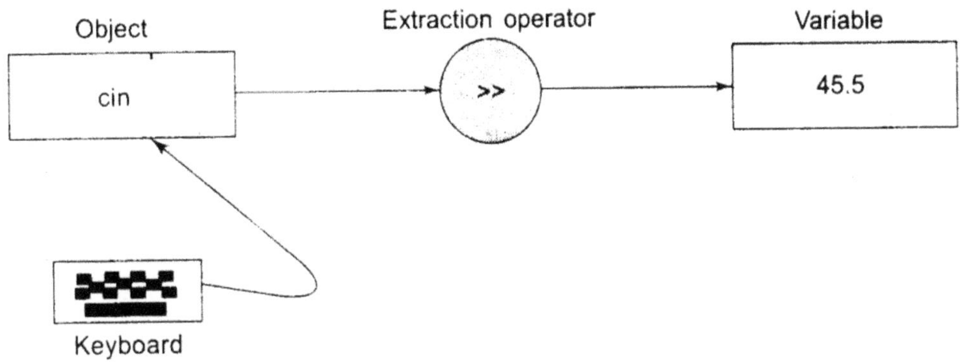

2) Output operator :

⇒ The output stream allows to perform writing operations on output devices such as screen, disk etc.

⇒ Output on the standard stream is performed using "cout" object.

⇒ C++ uses the bit-wise left-shift operator for performing console output operation. The syntax for the standard output stream operation is as follows :

cout << variable;

⇒ the word "cout" is followed by the symbole "<<" (insertion or put to operator) and then with the items (variables / constants / expressions) that are to be output.

⇒ The object "cout" must be associated with at least one argument. Like printf(), a constant value can also be sent as an argument the "cout" object.

⇒ "<<" operator sends the content of the variable on it's right side to the object on it's left side.

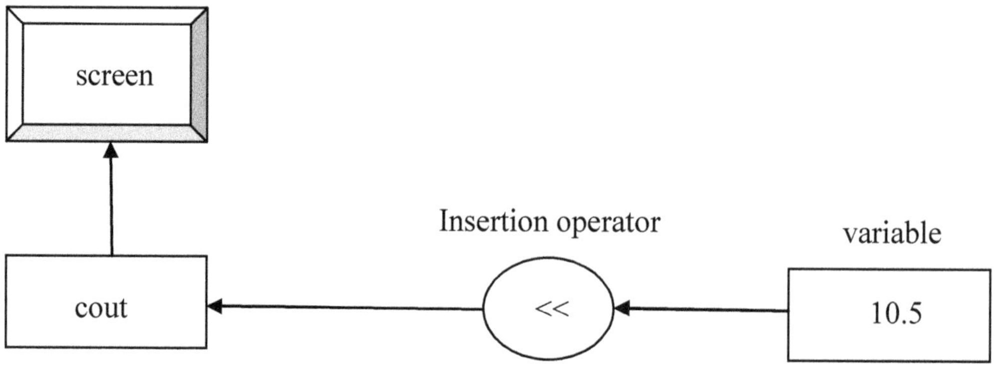

UNIT-2

TOKENS, EXPRESSIONS AND CONTROL STRUCTURE

2.1 Tokens :

⇒ The smallest individual units in a program are known as Tokens. Small tokens make your program/ build your program. C++ has following tokens:

⇒ A C++ program is written using these tokens, white spaces and the syntax of the language.

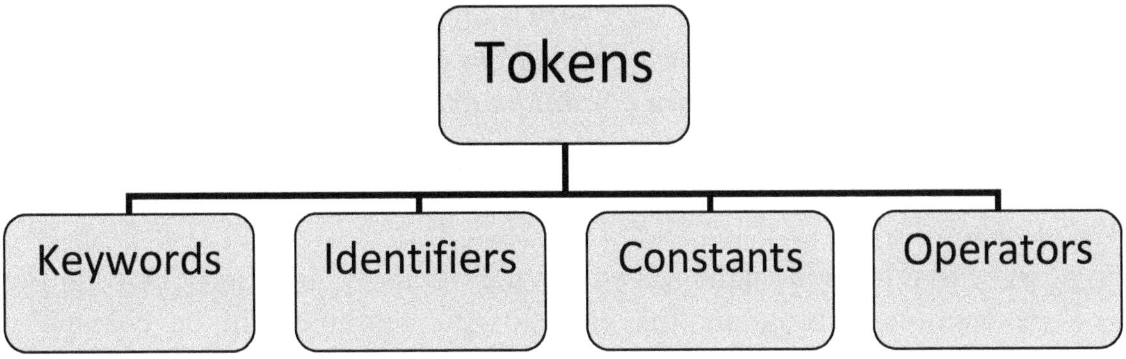

Keywords :

⇒ The keywords implement specific C++ language features. They are explicitly reserved identifiers and cannot be used as names for the program variables or other user-defined program implements.

⇒ The keywords have the pre-defined meanings and cannot be changed by the user.

⇒ The keywords are also known as "Reserved words" because their meaning is already explain to the compiler.

⇒ The given table gives the list of the keywords available in C++, but most of them are common to both C and C++.

asm	double	new	switch
auto	else	operator	template
break	enum	private	this
case	extern	protected	throw
catch	float	public	try
char	for	register	typedef
class	friend	return	union
const	goto	short	unsigned
continue	if	signed	virtual
default	inline	sizeof	void
delete	int	static	volatile
do	long	struct	while

Identifiers :

- In a C++ program, every word can be either classified as an identifier or keyword.
- As the name suggests, identifiers are used to identify or name of variables, symbolic constants, functions and so on.
- They are the fundamental requirement of any language. Each language has its own rules for naming these identifiers. The following rules are common to both C and C++.
    1) ***Only alphabetic characters, digits and underscores are permitted.***
    2) ***The name cannot start with a digit.***
    3) ***Uppercase and lowercase letters are distinct.***
    4) ***A declared keyword cannot be used as a variable name.***
    5) ***Must not contain any white space.***

Variables:

- A variable is a name given to the memory location. During the execution of program, the value of the variable will be changed / altered.

Constants :

- Constants refer to the fixed values that do not change during the execution of program.

Data types :

- The pre-defined identification of any variable is known as data type.
- C++ supports wide variety of data types and the programmer can select the type appropriate to the need of the application.
- C++ supports the following data types :
    1) ***Primary (fundamental) Data Types***
    2) ***Derived Data Type***
    3) ***User-Defined Data Type.***

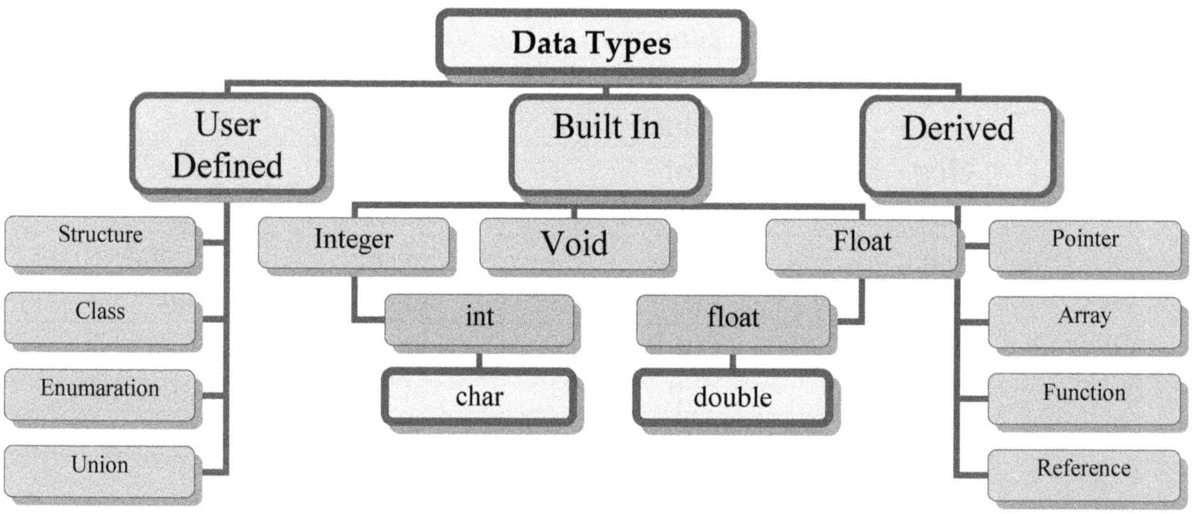

User-Defined Data Types :

Structure :

- A structure is a collection of elements having different data types.
- Structures help to organize complex data in a more meaningful way.
- It is also known as constructed data type that can handle a group of logically related data items.
  - ❖ **Syntax :**

```
Struct <tag_name>
{
        data type member-1;
        data type member-2;
        ................
        ................
};
```

  - ❖ **Example :**

```
Struct stud
{
        int no;
        char name[15];
}
```

- From the above syntax, we can see that the structure can be defined by the keyword "struct" followed by structure name.

Class :

- C++ permits us to define another user-defined data type known as "class". This can be used just like any other basic data type, to declare variables.
- The class variables are known as objects, which are the central focus of OOP.
- We can define the class by using the keyword "class".
  - **Syntax :**

```
Class <class name>
{
        // data members
        // member functions
}
```

  - **Example :**

```
Class student
{
        int age;
        public:


        void age()
```

```
        {
            cout<<"Enter Age :";
            cin>> age;
        }
};
int main()
{
        student s;
        s.age();
}
```

Enumeration:

- An enumerated data type is another user-defined type which provides a way for attaching names to numbers, thereby increasing comprehensibility of the code.
- To enumerate a list of words by assigning them values 0,1,2 and so on… the keyword "enum" is used.
- The syntax of enum statement is similar to the struct statement.
    - **Syntax :**

```
        Enum <tag name>
        { value1, value2, value 3}
```

    - **Example :**

```
Enum shape
{ circle , rectangle , triangle };
int main()
{
        int code;
        cout <<"Enter shape code :";
        cin>>code;
        switch(code)
        {
                case circle :
                cout<<"You select Circle..";
                break;
                case rectangle :
                cout<<"You select Rectangle..";
                break;
                case triangle :
                cout<<"You select Triangle..";
                break;
        }
return 0;
}
```

Union :

- Unions are concept that borrowed from structures and therefore follow the same syntax as structure.
- There is a major distinct between structure and union is that…..
- In structure, each member has it's own storage location, where as all members of a union use the same location.
- That means, union may contain many members of different types, it can handle only one member at a time.
  - **Syntax :**

```
Union <tag name>
{
        data type member-1;
        data type member-2;
        ………………
        ………………...
} variable of union type;
```

  - **Example :**

```
Union item
{
        int i_cd;
        char i_nm[25];
}itm;
```

2.2 Data Types

Primary Data types(Built-In Data Types) :

⇒ Primary data types are also known as "built-in" data types.

⇒ C++ supports the following basic data types.

Data type	Description
Char	A single byte that can hold one character.
Int	An integer number
Float	A single precision floating point number
Double	A double precision floating point number.

These basic data types may have several modifiers preceding them to serve the needs of various situations.

For Example…..

- The modifiers signed, unsigned applied to a character as well as integers and short, long may be applied to integers and long may be applied to a double.
- The table given below represents all the data types with modifiers….

Type	Bytes	Range
Char	1	-128 to 127
Unsigned char	1	0 to 255
Signed char	1	-128 to 127
Int	2	-32768 to 32767
Unsigned int	2	0 to 65535
Signed int	2	-32768 to 32767
Short int	2	-32768 to 32767
Unsigned short int	2	0 to 65535
Signed short int	2	-32768 to 32767
Long int	4	-2147483648 to 2147483647
Signed long int	4	-2147483648 to 2147483647
Unsigned long int	4	0 to 4294967295
Float	4	3.4e-38 to 3.4e+38
Double	8	1.7e-308 to 1.7e+308
Long double	10	3.4e-4932 to 1.1e+4932

Derived Data Types :

⇒ Generally the derived data types are derived by users to fulfill the needs of program.

⇒ Given below are the "Derived Data Types" available in C++.

1) Array :

- An array is a collection of elements having a similar data type.
- An array may be single dimensional or multi dimensional of any data type.
- The application of arrays in C++ is similar to that in C. The only exception is the way character arrays are initialized.
- When initializing a character array in ANSI C, the Compiler will allow us to declare the array size as the exact length of the string constant.

  For Example :

  char str[3]="xyz"; // is invalid for C++.

  Char str[4]="xyz"; // is valid for C++.

- That means, in C++ while declaring a character array, the size of the array must be one larger than the actual size, the programmer intends to leave out the character \0 (null) in the definition.

2) Functions :

- A function is a self contained block of statements that perform a particular task. Functions play an important role in program development.

- Dividing a program into functions is the major principles of top-down structured programming.
- With the help of functions, it is possible to reduce the size of program by calling and using them at different places into the program.
- C++ functions can be overload, to make it perform different tasks depending on the arguments passed to it.

3) Pointers :

- Pointer is defined as a variable used to make store memory address.
- It is similar to any other variable and has to be defined before using it to hold an address.
- (*) sign is used to declare a pointer variable.
- C++ adds two concepts about a pointer :
    1) **Constant Pointer**
    2) **Pointer to constant**

1) Constant Pointer :

- One cannot modify the address of constant pointer.

  For Example :

  Char *const ptr1="Good";

2) Pointer to Constant :

- The contents of what it points to cannot be changed.

  For Example:

  Int m=10;

  Int const *ptr2=&m;

Reference Variable :

- C++ introduces a new kind of variable known as a "Reference variable".
- C++ supports one more type of variable called reference variable, in addition to the value variable and pointer variables of C.
- Value variables are used to hold some numeric values; pointer variables are used to hold the address of some other value variables.
- Reference variable behaves similar to both, a value variable and a pointer variable.
- Thus, the reference variable enjoys the simplicity of value variables and power of the pointer variable.
- A reference variable provides an "alias" (or we can say that an "Alternative Name") for previously defined variable.
    - **Syntax :**

      Data type &reference variable name=value / variable name;
    - **Example :**

      int m;

      int &n=m; // here n is a reference variable of m.
- A reference variable must be initialized at the time of declaration.

- The initialization of a reference variable is completely different from assignment to it.

  Example program :

```
#include<iostream.h>
#include<conio.h>
int main()
{
        int x=10;
        int &y=x;
        cout<<"x="<<x;
        cout<<"y="<<y;
        y=y+10;
        cout<<"x="<<x;
        cout<<"y="<<y;
        getch();
        return 0;
}
```

- The above example shows that if you change the reference variable, the value variable will automatically changed and visa versa, because both variables access the same memory location.
- A major application of reference variable is in passing arguments to the functions.

Dynamic Initialization of Variable:

- Compiler would fix the initialization code at the time of compilation. However c++ permits initialization of the variables at run time. And this concept is referred to as "Dynamic Initialization of Variable".
- In C++, a variable can be initialized at run time using an expression at the place of declaration.
- For eg : int n=strlen(string);
- This statement is similar to

```
Int n;
N=strlen(string);
```

- Here both, the declaration and initialization of a variable can be done simultaneously at the place where the variable is used for the first time.
    - **Example :**

```
#include<iostream.h>
int main()
{
        char *s;
        cout<<"Enter String :";
        cin>>s;
        int len=strlen(s); // Dynamic Initialization ....
        Cout<<"length is : "<<len;
```

```
        Getch();
        Return 0;
    }
```

Type compatibility :

- C++ is very strict about the type compatibility as compared to C.
  For Example …
  C++ defines in, short int and log int as three different data type. They must be cast when their values are assigned to one another.
- In C++, the types of values must be the same for compatibility, or else, a cast must be applied.
- These restrictions are necessary in c++ in order to support function overloading where two functions with the same name are distinguished using the type of function argument.
- Another notable difference is the way char constants are stored. In c, they are stored as ints, and therefore …

  Sizeof('x') is equivalent to sizeof(int) in C.
- In C++ char is not promoted to the size of int, therefore,

  Sizeof('x') equals to size of (char)

2.3 Operators in C++ :

Scope Resolution Operator :

- Blocks and scopes can be used in constructing programs. We know that same variable name can be used to have different meanings in different blocks.
- The scope of the variable extends from the point of its declaration till the end of the block containing the declaration.

  Example :

  The two declaration of variable 'x' refer to two different memory location containing different values.

```
…………….
…………….
{
    int x = 10;
    ………..
    ………..
            {
            int x = 1;
            ……….
            ……….                Block-2          Block-1
            }
    ………..
}
```

- Here block-1 contains the block-2. note that a declaration in an inner block hides the declaration of the same variable in an outer block and therefore each declaration of 'x' causes a different data object.
- In C, global version of a variable cannot be accessed from within the inner block.
- C++ resolves this problem by introducing a new operator,
  That is.......

  :: (Scope Resolution Operator).
- This can be used to uncover a hidden variable.
- The general form is :

:: variable name

- In short, the scope resolution operator allows accessing the global version of the variable.
- There are total three uses of scope resolution operator.
  1) ***Used to access global version of variable.***
  2) ***Used to define the member function outside the class.***
  3) ***Used to call the static member function of a class.***

Example 1: Shows how access the global version of variable.

/* A program using scope resolution operator that shows how to access the global variable */

```
#include<conio.h>
#include<iostream.h>
int a=10;
int main()
{
        int b=20,a=30;
        clrscr();
        cout<<"\n Value of a : "<<a;
        cout<<"\n Value of ::a : "<<::a;
        cout<<"\n Value of b : "<<b;
        {
                int b=40;
                cout<<"\n Inner Block ";
                cout<<"\n Value of b : "<<b;
                cout<<"\n Value of ::a : "<<::a;
        }
        cout<<"\n Come Back in the main() ";
        cout<<"\n Value of a : "<<a;
        cout<<"\n Value of ::a : "<<::a;
        getch();
        return 0;
```

```
}
```

Example -2 : Shows how to define a member function outside the class.
/* A program using scope resolution operator that show how to define a member function outside the class */

```
#include<conio.h>
#include<iostream.h>

class Test
{
        int a,b;
        public:
                void getdata();
                void putdata();
};
void Test :: getdata()
{
        cout<<"Enter A :";
        cin>>a;
        cout<<"Enter B :";
        cin>>b;
}
void Test :: putdata()
{
        cout<<"Value of A is :"<<a;
        cout<<"value of B is :"<<b;
}
int main()
{
        Test t;
        clrscr();
        t.getdata();
        t.putdata();
        getch();
        return 0;
}
```

Example-3 : Shows how it can be used with the static members of the class.
/* A program using scope resolution operator that shows how to define and call the static members of a class. */

```
#include<conio.h>
#include<iostream.h>
```

```
class Test
{
        int code;
        static int count;
        public :
                void setcode()
                {
                        code=++count;
                }
                void showcode()
                {
                        cout<<"Object no :"<<code<<endl;
                }
                static void display()
                {
                        showcount();
                }
                static void showcount()
                {
                        cout<<"Count : "<<count<<endl;
                }
};
int Test ::count;
int main()
{
        Test t1,t2;
        clrscr();
        t1.setcode();
        t2.setcode();
        Test :: showcount();
        Test t3;
        t3.setcode();
        Test :: display();
        t1.setcode();
        t2.setcode();
        t3.setcode();
        getch();
        return 0;
}
```

Memory management operators :

- C++ supports two unary operators called new and delete that performs the task of allocating and freeing the memory dynamically.
- The memory management operators are also known as “Free Store Operators”.

- An object can be created using a new operator and destroyed using a delete operator. Thus, the life time of an object is directly under our control and is unrelated to the block structure of program.

NEW OPERATOR

- The new operator can be used to create an object of any type. It takes the following general form:
    - **Syntax :**

      Pointer variable= new data type;

    - **Example :**
      1) int *p=new int; // creates memory block of 2 bytes dynamically.
      2) float *f ;

         f = new float; // creates memory block of 2 bytes dynamically.
- We can also initialize the memory using new operator. This takes following form:
    - **Syntax:**

      Pointer variable=new data type(value);

      Here, the value specifies the initial value.
    - **Example :**

      Int *p =new int(10);

      Float *q=new float(5.4);
- New can be used to create a memory space for any data type include user defined type. Such as arrays, structures and classes.

  For example :

  Defining an array using new operator :
    - **Syntax :**

      Pointer variable=new data type[size];

      Here, size specifies the no. of elements in an array.
    - **Example :**

      int *p = new int[10];

  Advantages of new operator over a malloc() function.
  1) It automatically computes the size of the data object, no need to specify the size of operator.
  2) It automatically returns the correct pointer type, that's why no need to use type cast.
  3) It is possible to initiate the object while creating the memory space.
  4) Like any other operator, new and delete can be overloaded.

DELETE OPERATOR :

- When a data object is no longer needed, it is destroyed to release the memory space for use. The general form is :
    - **Syntax :**

      Delete pointer-variable;

Where,

Pointer variable is the pointer that points to a data object created with **new.**

- **Example :**
  Delete p;
  Delete f;

- If we want to delete/ free dynamically allocated array, we must use the following form of delete.
  - **Syntax :**
    Delete [size] pointer variable;
- The size specifies the no. of elements in the array to be freed. Some times there is no need to specify the size of array.
  - **Example :**
    Delete []p;
    Will delete the entire array pointed to by p.

Type casting :

- C++ permits explicit type conversion of variables or expression using the type cast operator.
  - **Syntax :**
    Type_name (expression)

  And we all know that ....

  (type name) expression // this is C notation.
  - **Example :**
    Average=sum/float(i);
- Here the type name behaves as if it is a function for converting values to a designated type.

Expressions and Their Types :

- An expression is a combination of operators, constants and variables arranged as per the rules of the language.
- It may also include function calls which return values. An expression may consist of one or more operands, and zero or more operators to produce a value.
- There are total seven types of Expression, they are as given below :

Expressions	Description	Example
Constant Expression	Consist of only constant values.	20+5 'a'
Integral Expression	This type of expressions is produce integer result after implementing all types of conversion.	A*B 10+int(3.0) m*n-2 no
Float Expression	This type of expressions is produce floating-point result	x+y x+float(10) 10.56

<table>
<tr><td></td><td>after implementing all types of conversion.</td><td>x+y/3</td></tr>
<tr><td>Pointer Expression</td><td>This type of expressions is produce address values.</td><td>&x
ptr+1
ptr</td></tr>
<tr><td>Relational Expression</td><td>This type of expressions gives a result of type bool which takes a value true or false.</td><td>x<=y
age==18
m+n>=100</td></tr>
<tr><td>Logical Expression</td><td>This type of expressions combines two or more relational expressions and produces bool type result.</td><td>a>b && a>c
x==10 || y==5</td></tr>
<tr><td>Bitwise Expression</td><td>This type of expressions is used to manipulate data at bit level. They are used for testing and shifting bits.</td><td>X<<3
y>>3
here x and y contains some value.</td></tr>
</table>

Special Assignment Expression :

- The assignment expression can be any one from the given three types.
    1) **Chained assignment**
    2) **Embedded Assignment**
    3) **Compound Assignment**

1) **Chained Assignment :**
    - A chained expression cannot be used to initialize variable at the time of declaration.

    Example :

    Float a=b=12.34; // this is illegal

    Instead of this you can write like this……

    Float a=12.34, b=12.34 // this is legal

2) **Embedded Assignment :**

    X= (y = 50) +10

    This statement is similar to …..

    Y=50;

    X=y+10;

    Here (y=50) is an assignment expression known as embedded assignment. Here, the value 50 is assigned to y and then the result 50+10 =60 is assigned to X.

3) **Compound Assignment :**

- Like C, C++ supports a compound assignment operator which is a combination of the assignment operator with arithmetic operator. For Example....
- The simple assignment

  no=no+10;

  may be written as

  no+=10;
- the operator += is known as compound assignment operator or short-hand assignment operator.

Manipulators :

- Manipulators are the operators that are used to format the data display. The most commonly used manipulators are **'setw'** and **'endl'**.

1) endl :

- This manipulator, when used in an output statement, causes a linefeed to be inserted.
- It has the same effect as using the new line character "\n".

  For example :

Use of "\n" character	Use of Endl Manipulator
cout<<"Hello World"; cout<<"\n Good Morning "; cout<<"\n Have a nice day";	cout<<"Hello World"<<endl; cout<<" Good Morning"<<endl; cout<<" Have a nice day"<<endl;

The above mentioned both the example gives you the same output.

2) Setw :

- This manipulator is used to specify common field width for all the numbers and force them to be printed right-justified.

  Syntax :

  Setw(width)

Example :

```
int x=123,y=45,z=34;
cout<<setw(5)<<x<<end;
cout<<setw(5)<<y<<endl;
cout<<setw(5)<<z<<endl:
```

Output

1	2	3
	4	5
	3	4

```
int x=123,y=45,z=34;
cout<<x<<end;
cout<<y<<endl;
cout<<z<<endl:
```

Output

1	2	3
4	5	
3	4	

.4 Control Structures :

- We all know that program is the set of statements that can execute normally in sequence one by one without skipping any statement.
- Now, if we want that our program execute only when the particular condition is satisfied. That means our program execution is on the basis of the conditions and some portion will be skipped and some portion will be executed, that is totally condition-based execution. That means you can change control flow of the program.
- To perform such things C++ supports decision making statements that are as given below:
    1) if statement
    2) switch statement
    3) Conditional operator statement
    4) *goto statement*
- These statements are purely known as "Decision Making". And they are also 'control' the flow of execution, they are also known as "Control Statement" / "Control Structure".

1) Decision Making With IF Statement :

- The if statement is the powerful decision making statement and is used to control the flow of execution of the statements. C++ uses the keyword if to implement the decision control instruction. It is basically a 2 way decision making statement.

  Syntax: -

  ```
  if(test expression)
  {
          statement block;
  }
  ```

- This structure allows the computer to evaluate the expressions first and then, depending on whether the expression will evaluate to true or not? Then depending on the result it will transfer the control on a particular statement.

- If the test expression is evaluated to true, then the statement-block will be executed. And the statement-x will also be executed.
- If the test condition is evaluated to false. Then the statement-block will be skipped and directly the control will move to the statement-x.
- Note that, In both the cases the statement-x will be executed.
- An Example of the simple if condition is as given below:

Example :-

```
If(age>=18)
{
        cout<<"You get License";
}
```

2) Decision making with IF...ELSE Statement :

- The if else statement is the extension of the simple if statement. The general form of if...else is as given below:

Syntax:

```
if(test expression)
{
        True-block statements;
}
else
{
        False-block statement;
}
Statement-x;
```

- The structure allows the expression to be evaluated first and depending on the value which is returned by the expression the control is transferred to a particular statement block.
- First the condition is evaluated; if the condition is true then the control is transferred to the True-block of the program, and then the statement-x will be executed, which is out of the if..else block.
- If the condition is false, then the control is transferred to the False-block of the program. And then the statement-x, which is out of the if..else block.
- Note that, the statement-x will be executed in both the cases, they are not related with the result of the condition.
- An Example of If...Else is as given below:

Example :

```
If(age>=18)
{
        cout<<"you get License";
}
else
{
        cout<<"you don't get License";
}
```

3) Decision making with nested if…else statement :

- When a one if..else statement is within the another if..else is known as "Nesting of If..Else". The general form of the nested if..else is as given below:
  Syntax: -

```
if(test expression-1)
{
        if(test expression-2)
        {
                statement-1;
        }
        else
        {
                statement-2;
        }
}
else
{
        statement-3;
}
Statement –x;
```

- In this case, the structure shows that a condition is evaluated first, then according to the condition the control will move in your program.
- If the Exp.1 evaluated to true, then the control will proceeds to the next expression, i.e Exp.2. If both the Expressions are evaluated to true then the statement-1 will be executed.
- If the Exp1 evaluated to true and Exp.2 evaluated to false then the control will transferred to the statemene-2.
- And if the Exp.1 will evaluated to false, the control will transferred to the else portion of the main condition. That means the statement-3 will be evaluated.

- And in any of the cases the control will proceeds always to the statement-x. which is not depend on the result of the condition.

Example:

```
if(a>b)
{
        if(a>c)
        cout<<"\n A is Big";
        else
        cout<<"\n C is Big";
}
else
{
        if(c>b)
        cout<<"\n C is Big";
        else
        cout"\n B is Big";
}
```

4) Decision making with else…if ladder :

- Just observe that the program uses the nested if-elses. This leads to three disadvantages:
    1) As the No. of conditions is going increased the level of indentation is also increased. An as a result the program is shifted to the right hand side, and readability of your program will be decreased.
    2) In case of nested if-else you must take care about the pair of the ifs and elses.
    3) You must take care of the opening braces and closing braces of each & every ifs and elses.
- There is one more way in which we can write the program of multiple conditions, This involves usage of else if blocks as shown below:

Syntax: -

```
if(condition-1)
        statement-1;
        else if (condition-2)
                statement-2;
                else if(condition-3)
                        statement-3;
                        else if (condition-n)
                                statement-n;
                                else
                                  default-statement;
statement-x;
```

- This construct is known as the "ELSE…IF LADDER".
- The conditions are evaluated from top to bottom, downwards.
- As soon as a true condition is found, the statement associated with that condition will be executed, and then the control will transferred to the statement-x.(by skipping the rest of ladders).
- When all the condition become false, then the else portion that is the final else that contains the default- statement will be executed, and the control will transferred at the statement-x.
- That means the program execution will become faster, when you are using the else…if ladder instead of more than one ifs. Because after execution of a particular statement, there is not more conditions are checking, that means skipping the rest of ladder.
- The example of the else if ladder is as give below:

Example :

```
if(per>=70)
{
        cout<<"\n You get Distinction";
}
else if (per>=60 && per<70)
{
cout<<"\n You get First Class";
}
else if(per>=50 &&per<60)
{
        cout<<"\n You get Second Class";
}
else if(per>=40 && per<50)
{
        cout<<"\n You get Pass Class";
}
else
{
        cout<<"\n You are FAIL";
}
```

5) Multi way decision with Switch statement :

We have already done the decision making using simple ifs and multiple ifs and elses, and as we know that each new form of if was reduced the limitations of previous one. Actually there is no limitation of if…..else ladder. But when the no. of conditions are going to increasing the level of indentation will also going to increasing, at that time even a designer of a program will confuse about the program. So remove this limitation of the else…if ladder, C provides a facility called the Switch-Case statement, also known as "Branching Statement". The syntax of the Switch is as given below:

Syntax: -

```
switch(expression)
{
        case value-1:
                        block-1;
                        break;
        case value-2:
                        block-2;
                        break;
        ..........
        ..........
        Default:
                        Default-block;
                        Break;
}
Statement-x;
```

- The switch statement is preticularly used for menu driven programming.
- The switch statement checks value of the expression against a list of case value, and when a match is found, a block of statements associated with that case is executed.
- The expression is an integer or character expressions.
- Value-1,value-2….are the integer constants or the character constants.
- Each value in the list of case must be unique, that means no 2 case have similar values.
- Not that, each case keyword with expression is followed by a colon.
- The block-1,block-2…. Are the statement blocks and may contain 1 or more statement that will be executed.

Example :

```
int main( )
{
        int ch,a,b;
        cout<<"\n 1.Addition";
        cout<<"\n 2.Subtraction";
        cout<<"\n 3. Multiplicatioin";
        cout<<"\n 4. Division";
        cout<<"\n Enter Your choice : ";
        cin>>ch;
```

```
        cout<<"\n Enter A & B :";
        cin>>a;
        cin>>b;
        switch(ch)
        {
                case 1:
                        c=a+b;
                        cout<<c;
                        break;
                case 2:
                        c=a-b;
                        cout<<c;
                        break;
                case 3:
                        c=a*b;
                        cout<<c;
                        break;
                case 4:
                        c=a/b;
                        cout<<c;
                        break;
                default:
                        cout<<"\n Invalid choice";
                        break;
        }
}
```

Looping Structure :

1) **Loop: -**
   - To perform a particular task no. of times the concepts of loops can be used. Loops can be of 2 types:
     1) **Finite Loop:**
        The loop in which the no. of iteration is predefined is known as Finite Loop.
     2) **Infinite Loop:**
        The loop in which the no. of iteration is not predefined is known as Infinite Loop.

2) **Iterations: -**
   - The meaning of the word "Iteration" is "Repetition".

3) **Counter Variable : -**
   - The variable which is used to count the no. of iterations is known as counter variable.

- In looping the sequence of statements are executed until some conditions for termination of the body of the loop are satisfied.
- Therefore the program loop is made up of 2 statements:
    1) The Body of the loop
    2) The Control statement (A Condition)
- Depending on the position of the condition (control statement) in the loop, the loop may be classified into 2 categories :
    1) ***Entry-Controlled loop***
    2) ***Exit-Controlled loop***
- There are 3 methods through which some part of the program can be repeated number of times, they are as given below:
    1) ***The while statement***
    2) ***The do…while statement***
    3) ***The for statement***

1) The while Statement :

- The while statement is the simplest of all the loop structure in the C language.
- The syntax of the while statement is as given below:

Syntax: -

```
while( test expression)
{
        body of the loop
}
statement-x;
```

- The while statement is known as entry-controlled loop. Because the condition is checked first and then the body of the loop will be executed if the condition is true.
- Here the while is the keyword which denotes that the following block is the loop.
- If test expression is evaluated to true then and then the body of the loop will be executed, otherwise the control will transfer to the statement-x, which is immediately after the loop.
- If the condition is true and the loop will executed, then again the condition will be checked if the condition is true than the body of the loop will be executed. This process is continued while the test condition is not evaluated to false.

Example: -

```
int main( )
{
        int no=1;
        while(no<=10)
        {
                cout"\n %d"<<no;
                no++;
```

```
}
getch( );retururn 0;
}
```

2) The Do...While Statement :

- The do…while statement is known as an “Exit-Controlled Loop”.
- In case of while loop, the condition is checked first and then the body of the loop will be executed. That means if the condition is not satisfied at first attempt then the control will jump out of the loop.
- Where as in case of do…while statement the body of the loop is executed first and then the condition will checked, that means the body of the loop is executed if a condition is not satisfied at first attempt.
- The syntax and example of the do…while statement is as given below:

  Syntax: -

```
do
{
        body of the loop
}
while (condition);
```

- In above syntax the do & while are the keywords which defines the loop.
- Consider the syntax the condition is not checked at the entry of the loop, but the condition is on exiting the loop.
- According to the syntax, when the control will be reached at the do statement, then the control will proceeds to the body of the loop. And at last the condition will check.
- Now if the condition is true then the control will go at the do statement again and the body of the loop is executed once again, this process continuous as long as the condition is true.

  Example:

```
int main( )
{
        int sum=0,count=1;
        do
        {
                sum=sum+count;
                count=count+1;
        }while(count<=10);
        cout“\n The Summation of 1 to 10 is : “<<sum;
        getch( );
        retuturn 0;
}
```

3) The For Statement :

- The for statement is the most widely looping control statement among the all statements. This is again an entry controlled looping statement and provides a more concise loop control structure.
- The for loop is very simple and the syntax of the for loop is something different from the other 2 statements.

  Syntax: -

  ```
  for (initialization ; test condition ;increment)
  {
  body of the loop;
  }
  ```

  Where,

  You can see the initialization of the counter variable is also the part of the loop.
- Here the for statement is consist of 3 parts:

  1) Initialization (i)
  2) Testing (t)
  3) Increment (i)
- The initialization of the counter variable is done only once, using an assignment statement.
- The second part is consist of the conditional statement, that is the used to control the loop. If you want to know the maximum iterations of the loop, then you can identify it using the conditional expression.
- The last part is consist of the increment or decrement of the counter variable, through which the value of the counter variable is finally reach at the maximum iterations of the loop.
- After executing this increment and decrement of the variable the value of the variable the new value of the variable is again tested, if the new value of the variable is satisfy the condition then the body of the loop is again executed. This process is continued till the value of the counter variable is reached at the maximum value of the variable.

  Example: -

  ```
  // A program that shows the use of the for loop.
  #include<stdio.h>
  #include<conio.h>
  void main( )
  {
          for(int i=1;i<=10;i++)
          {
          cout<<"\n Computer";
          }
  getch( );
  }
  ```

UNIT-3

FUNCTIONS IN C++

3.1 Introduction to Functions:

- We know that functions play an important role in program development.
- Dividing a program into functions is one of the major principles of top-down, structured programming.
- Another advantage of using functions is that it is possible to reduce the size of a program by calling and using them at different places in the program.

Elements of Function:

- In order to make use of an user defined function, we need to established three elements that are related to function :
  1. **Function Declaration or prototype**

     Syntax :

     Return data type Function Name (Parameter List);

     Example :

     ```
     int sum(int, int);
     ```
  2. **Function call**

     Syntax :

     Function name(Parameter list);

     Example :

     ```
     ans = sum(a, b);
     ```
  3. **Function definition (function declaration and a function body)**

     Syntax :

     ```
     Return data type Function Name (Parameter List)
     {
             Local variable declaration;
             Statements 1;
             Statement 2 ;
             --------------
             --------------
             Return (expression);
     }
     ```

     Example :

     ```
     int sum(int x, int y)
     {
             int ans = x + y ;
             return (ans);
     }
     ```

The main() Function :

- C does not specify return type for the main() function which is the starting point for the execution of a program. The definition of main() would like this :

```
main()
{
        //main program statements
}
```

- This is perfectly valid because the main() in c does not return any value.
- In c++, the main() returns a value of type int to the operating system. C++, therefore explicitly defines main() as matching one of the following prototypes :

```
int main();
int main (int argc, char * argv[]);
```

- The functions that have a return value should use the return statement for termination.
- The main() function in C++ is, therefore, defined as follows :

```
int main()
{
        .........
        .........
        return 0;
}
```

- Since the return type of functions is int by default, the keyword int in the main() header is optional. Most C++ compilers will generate an error or warning if there is no return statement. Turbo C++ issues the warning

Function should return a value

- And then proceeds to compile the program. It is good programming practice to actually return a value from main( ).

3.2 Function Prototyping :

- Function prototyping is one of the major improvements added to C++ functions. The prototype describes the function interface to the compiler by giving details such as the number and types of arguments and the type of the return values.
- With function prototyping, a template is always used when declaring and defining a function.
- When a function is called, the compiler uses the template to ensure that proper arguments are passed, and return value is treated correctly.
- Any violation in matching the arguments or the return types will be caught by the compiler at the time of compilation itself. These checks and controls did not exist in the conventional C function.
- Function prototype is a "Declaration Statement" in the calling program and is of the following form :
    - **type function-name (argument-list);**
- The argument-list contains the types and names of arguments that must be passed to the function

  Example :

float volume(int x, float y, float z)

- Note that each argument variable must be declared independently inside the parentheses. That is, a combined declaration like ……

float volume (int x, float y,z); // this is illegal.

- In the function declaration, the names of the arguments are dummy variables and therefore they are optional. That is, the form

float volume (int, float, float);

- Is acceptable at the place of declaration. At this stage, the compiler checks for the type of arguments when the function is called.
- In general, we can either include or exclude the variable names in the argument list of prototypes. The variable names in the prototype just act as placeholders and therefore if names are used, they don't have to match the names used in the ***function-call*** **or** ***function definition.***
- In the function definition, names are required because the arguments must be referenced inside the function.

Example:

```
float volume(int a, int b, float c)
{
        float v=a*b*c;
        …………
        …………
}
```

- The function volume() can be invoked in a program as follows :

float cube1=volume(b1,w1,h1); //function call

- The variable b1, w1, and h1 are known as the actual parameters which specify the dimensions of cube1. Their types (which have been declared earlier) should match with the types declared in the prototype. Remember, the calling statement should not include type names in the argument list.
- We can aloes declare a function with an ***empty argument list***, as in the following example.

void display();

- In c++, this means that the function does not pass any parameters. It is identical to the statement.

void display(void);

Call By Reference:

- In traditional C, a function call passes arguments by value. The called function creates a new set of variables and copies the values of arguments into them. The function does not have access to the actual variables in the calling program and can only work on the copies of values.
- This mechanism is fine if the function does not need to alter the values of the original variables in the calling program.

- But, there may arise situations where we would like to change the values of variables in the calling program.
- Provision of **reference variables** in C++ permits us to pass parameters to the functions by reference. When we pass arguments by reference, the 'formal' arguments in the called function become aliases to the 'actual' arguments in the calling function. This means that when the function is working with its own arguments, it is actually working on the original data.
- In short, we can achieve the call by reference mechanism via **"Reference variable"**.
- **Syntax :**

  Return type function_name(datatype &arg1, datatype &arg2);

Example : This example shows call by reference mechanism using Reference Variable:

```
#include<iostream.h>
#include<conio.h>
void swap(int &, int &);
int main()
{
        int a,b;
        cout<<"\n Enter First value :";
        cin>>a;
        cout<<"\n Enter Second value :";
        cin>>b;
        swap(a,b);
        cout<<"After Swaping values...";
        cout<<"A="<<a;
        cout<<"B="<<b;
        getch();
        return 0;
}
void swap(int &x, int &y)
{
        int temp;
        temp=x;
        x=y;
        y=temp;
}
```

Note :

- ✓ From the above example program, you can see that variable x and y becomes the aliases of the variable a and b.
- ✓ Once they become reference of a and b, now you can access those variable by the names x and y or may be a and b.

- ✓ So when you perform the swapping operation in the function, that operation performs on a and b variable.

Return By Reference :

- A function that returns a reference variable is actually an alias for the referred variable.
- The method of returning a reference variable is used in operator overloading.

```
#include<iostream.h>
#include<conio.h>
int & max (int &x, int &y);        //prototype
int main()
{
        int a,b;
        clrscr();
        cout<<"Enter First value :";
        cin>>a;
        cout<<"Enter Second value :";
        cin>>b;
        max(a,b)=425;
        cout<<"After Execution of max()... "<<endl;
        cout<<"Value of A is : "<<a<<endl;
        cout<<"Value of B is : "<<b<<endl;
        getch();
        return 0;
}
int & max(int &x, int &y)
{
        if(x>y)
                return x;
        else
                return y;
}
```

Inline Function :

- To reduce the cost of calls to small functions, C++ supports a new feature called "Inline Function".
- An inline function is a function that expanded "**in line**" when it is called.
- The compiler replaces the function call with the corresponding function code (something similar to macros expression).

Syntax:

```
inline function-header
{
    function body
}
```

Example :

```
inline float area(float r)
{
        return (3.14*r*r);
}
```

- It is easy to make a function inline; just we have to specify the keyword **"inline"**, to the function definition.
- All inline function must be defined before they are called.
- Remember that, the inline keyword merely sends a request, not a command, to the compiler.
- **Where inline expression may not work?**
    1. For functions returning values, if a loop, a switch, or goto exist.
    2. For functions not returning values, if a return statement exist.
    3. If function contains static variable.
    4. If inline functions are recursive.
- The inline functions take more memory, when the statements define the inline functions are reproduced every time a function call is made.
- So if the statements in the inline functions are on higher side, use of inline function may be costly in terms of memory.

Example : A program using an inline function.

```
#include<iostream.h>
#include<conio.h>
inline float multi(float x, float y) //inline function
{
        return x*y;
}
inline double div(double p, double q)  //inline function
{
        return p/q;
}
int main()
{
        int a=12.345;
        int b=9.82;
        cout<<endl<<multi(a,b);
        cout<<endl<<div(a,b);
        getch();
        return 0;
}
```

Default Argument :

- An argument value that is spcified in a function declaration and is used if the corresponding actual argument is omitted when the function is called.
- C++ allows us to call a function without specifying all it's arguments.
- In such cases, the function assigns a default value to the parameter which does not have matching argument in the function call.

- Default values are specified when the function is declared.
- For Example ….

  float amt(float p_amt, int period, float rate=0.15);

  The above prototype declares a default value of 0.15 to the argument rate. So, function call like…….val=amt(500,7);
- A default argument is checked for type at the time of declaration and evaluated at the time of call.
- Note : only the trailing arguments can have default values and therefore we must add defaults from right to left.

int add(int i, int j=5, int k=10); int add(int i=2, int j=5, int k=10);	int add(int i, int j=5, int k=10); int add(int i=2, int j=5, int k=10);

- Default arguments are useful in situations where some arguments always have the same value.
- **Use of default argument :**
  1. **We can use default arguments to add new parameters to the existing functions.**
  2. **Default arguments can be used to combine similar functions into one.**

  Example :

```
#include<iostream.h>
#include<conio.h>
void printline(char ch='$', int len=40);
int main()
{
        clrscr();
        printline();
        cout<<"\n Hello World"<<endl;
        printline('*',35);
        cout<<"\n Hello…"<<endl;
        printline('@');
        getch();
        return 0;
}
void printline(char ch, int len)
{
        for(int i=1; i<=len; i++)
        {
                cout<<ch;
        }
}
```

Const Argument :

- In C++, an argument to a function can be declared as const as shown below.

- For example...

```
Int strlen(const char *p);
Int length(const string &s);
```

- Here, the qualifier const tells the compiler that the function should not modify the argument.
- The compiler will generate an error when this condition is violated.
- Constant argument is significant only when we pass arguments by reference or pointer.

Example Program:

```
#include<iostream.h>
#include<conio.h>
void print_string(const char ch[], int no);
int main()
{
        char *ch;
        clrscr();
        cout<<"Enter String : ";
        cin>>ch;
        print_string(ch, 5);
        getch();
        return 0;
}
void print_string(const char ch[], int no)
{
        for(int i=0; i<no; i++)
        {
                cout<<ch<<endl;
        }
}
```

Function overloading :

- **Overloading :** overloading refers to the use of the same thing for different purposes.
- In C++, a function can be overloaded, that is same function name can be used multiple times to perform different tasks.
- This terminology is termed as...Function Overloading.
- The "function overloading" mechanism is useful to achieve the "Polymorphism".
- Using the concepts of function overloading, one can define a family of functions with one common name, but different argument lists.
- Working of function overloading..
- In order to invoke appropriate function from the given functions, the compiler matches the arguments with the function call and executes the statements in the functions.
- The correct function invoked is determined by verifying the argument type, ot the number of arguments.

- For Example :
```
int add(int a, int b);
float add(float a, float b);
float add(int a, float b);
```
- When function call is made, first it matches the prototype and then calls the appropriate function for execution.
- In order to match the appropriate function the following steps are followed.
- The compiler first tries to find an exact match and then uses the function.
- If an actual match is not found, the compiler uses the integral promotions to actual arguments such as char to int and float to double.
- Even when the above steps fail, the compiler tries to use the built-in Conversions and then uses the functions. If there are multiple matches for conversion then the compiler generates an error message.
- If all the above steps fail, then the compiler tries the user-defined conversion in combination with integral promotions and built-in conversions to find match.
- **Example :**

```
#include<iostream.h>
#include<conio.h>
int volume(int);
double volume(double, int);
long volume(long, int ,int);
int main()
{
        cout<<volume(10)<<endl;
        cout<<volume(2.5,8)<<endl;
        cout<<volume(100L,75,15)<<endl;
        getch();
        return 0;
}
int volume(int x)
{
        return (x*x*x);
}

double volume(double r,int h)
{
        return (3.14519*r*r*h);
}

long volume(long l, int b, int h)
{
        return(l*b*h);
}
```

UNIT - 4
CLASSES AND OBJECTS

Introduction:

- The ability to create a class in C++ is the most important enhancement that was made to the C language.
- 'class' is the most important feature of C++.
- C++ was originally called 'C with classes'.
- Class was extended from C structure.

C structures revisited:

- Structure is the unique feature of 'C' language.
- A structure is a convenient tool for handling a group of logically related data items.
- A structure in a 'C' is a collection of similar or dissimilar data types.
- Just like a built-in type declaration we can create variables of structure type after structure once defined.

  For Example :

```
struct stud
{
        int rollno;
        char name[20];
        int age;
        char address[40];
};
```

In above example

```
struct                      → keyword
stud                        → Name of structure
rollno, name,age,address    → structure members or elements
```

- Now we can create variables of type stud like this:

  struct stud s; **// C declaration**

  stud s; **//C++ declaration**

- Member variable can be accessed using the dot or period(.) operator as follows:

  s.rollno=1;

  strcpy(s.name,"Virani");

- Structure can have arrays, pointers or structure as members.

Limitations of c structures:

- The standard c does not allow the struct data type to be treated like built-in types.
- For example, consider following structure

```
struct sub
{
        int c;
        int foxpro;
};
void main()
{
        Struct sub s1,s2,s3;
        s1.c=50;
        s1.foxpro=60;
        s2.c=60;
        s2.foxpro=50;
        s3=s1+s2;
}
```

Here we have assigned value to s1 and s2. Now,

S3=s1+s2;

is not possible. So we cannot add two subjects and cannot subtract one from other.

- Another limitation of c structure is that they do not permit data hiding. As all members of structure are public. So structure members can be directly accessed by structure variable by any function anywhere in their scope.

Structure in C++:

- C++ supports all the features of structure as defined in c.
- In C++ structure provides the facility to hide data.(Private member).
- Structure supports inheritance.
- Structure can have both variables and functions as members.
- In structure one can declare some of its members as 'private'.
- So that it cannot be accessed directly by external function (non member function).
- In C++ structure name are stand-alone, so keyword struct can be omitted in declaration of structure variable.

  For example :

```
struct stud s; // C declaration
stud s ;       //C++ declaration
```

Class & Structure:

- Class contains all the features of structure.
- The only difference between a structure and a class in c++ is that by default all members are public in structure and private in class.
- Most of C++ programmers use structure for holding only data and class to hold both the data and function.

Class and object:

- Before going through class lets again revise an object.

  Object:
  - "An object is a real word entity."
  - An object is simply something that is relevant to particular application.
    For example,
    We want to generate student's result, and then here student is an object.
  - Each object has state and behavior.

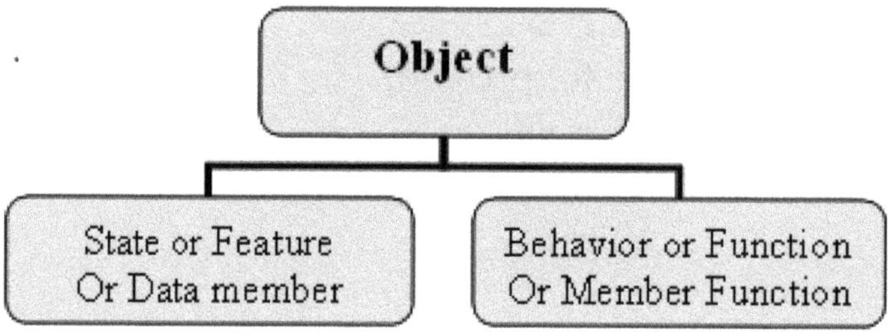

  - Here, state of object menace feature of an object which is represented by data members. And behavior means functionality of an object which is represented by member function. A class is mould which defines all data members and methods that object should have.
    For example,
    Object → Car
    Features → Color, Manufacturer, Size
    Functions → Run

  Class:
  - "A class is a mould or template or blueprint of an object."
  - Class defines all data members and methods that an object should have.
  - It is a way to bind the data and its associated function together.
  - It defines the characteristics the object will process.
  - A class is an expanded concept of a data structure: instead of holding only data, it can hold both data and functions.
  - An object is an instantiation of a class. In terms of variables, a class would be the type, and an object would be the variable.
  - Class is created using the keyword class. A class declaration defines a new type that links a code and data .This new type is then used to declare objects of that class.

Class Specification:

- A class specification has two parts

1) Class declaration.
2) Class function definition.

- General form of class declaration is:

```
class class-name
{
        private data and function
        access-specifier:
        data and function
        access-specifier:
        data and function
                ………….
        …………………
}object list;
```

- Where class_name is a valid identifier for the class.
- object_names is an optional list of names for objects of this class.
- The body of the declaration can contain members, that can be either data or function declarations, and optionally access specifiers.
- Access specifier is one of these three C++ keywords:

  (1) Private.
  (2) Public.
  (3) Protected.

Private:

- By default, function and data declared within a class are private to that class and may be accessed only by other members of the same class or from their friends.

Public:

- The public access-specifier allows function or data to be accessible from anywhere where the object is visible.

Protected:

- The protected access specifier is needed when inheritance is involved. Protected members are accessible from members of their same class and from their friends, but also from members of their derived classes.

Note :
By default, all members of a class declared with the class keyword have private access for all its members. Therefore, any member that is declared before one other class specifier automatically has private access.

Data Hiding:

- Private access specifier is used in C++ to implement a concept of data hiding. It means that data is hidden (canceled) within a class, so that it cannot be accessed by function outside the class even by mistake.

Member Function or Method:

- Functions that are declared within a class are called member function or method.
- Member function may access any elements (data or functions) of the class of which they are part. It includes all private data elements.

Member Variables:

- Variables that are declared inside a class are called member variables or data member or instance variable.
- So, any element of a class can be referred to as a member of a class. Achieve an encapsulation we should make all data members of a class private to that class.

  For example :

```
class stud
{
  //by default private
        int no;
        char name[20];
        int total;
  public:
        void get_data()
        {
                cout<<"\n\n\nEnter No:";
                cin>>no;
                cout<<"\nEnter Name:";
                cin>>name;
                cout<<"\nEnter Total:";
                cin>>total;
        }

        void put_data()
        {
                cout<<"\n\n\nNo:"<<no;
                cout<<"\nName:"<<name;
                cout<<"\nTotal:"<<total;
                float per=total/5;
                cout<<"\nPercentage:"<<per;
        }
};


int main( )
{
        stud s;
        s.get_data( );
```

```
        s.put_data( );
        return(0);
    }
```

Private data members (By default private) → no,name,age

Public member function → get_data(),put_data()

Creating object:

- In C++ class variables are known as objects. Once a class variable of that class has been created we can create variable of that type using class name.
  For example :
  stud s;
- Here **stud** is class name and **s** is object. Above statement will create memory for **s**. We can say that **s** is object of class **stud**.
- Another way to create object is

```
class stud
{
    ...........
} s1, s2, s3;
```

Note: ***Class specification, like a structure provides only a template and does not create any memory space for object.***

Objects and Instances :

- There is a very important distinction between an object and an instance of an object. An object is actually a definition, or a template for instances of that object. An instance of an object is an actual thing that can be manipulated.
- For example, we could define a Person object, which may include such member data as hair color, eye color, height, weight, etc. An instance of this object could be "Mihir" and Mihir has values for hair color, eye color, etc. This allows for multiple instances of an object to be created.

Accessing class members:

- Member functions have only right to access private data of a class. With the help of member function objects can communicate by sending and receiving message.
  object-name. function-name (actual arguments);
  For example :
  s1.get_data ();
  s1.put_data ();
  It is illegal to call private member of class
  s1.no=1;
  We can call public members of class through object.
  For example :

```
class stud
{
```

```
        int no;
        public:
        char name[20];
        int age;
    };
    stud s1;
    s1.age=20;
```

Defining member function:

- We can define member function in two ways.
  1) Inside the class definition.
  2) Outside the class definition.

1) Inside the class definition:

- One method of defining a member function is to replace the function declaration by actual function definition inside the class.
- A function which is defined inside a class is treated as an **inline function**. So all restrictions and limitations of inline function is also applicable here. Normally only small functions are defined inside the class definition.

For example :

```
class stud
{
        int no;
        char name[20];
        int age;
  public:
        void get_data()
        {
                cout<<"\n\n\nEnter No:";
                cin>>no;
                cout<<"\nEnter Name:";
                cin>>name;
                cout<<"\nEnter Total:";
                cin>>total;
        }
        void put_data()
        {
                cout<<"\n\n\nNo:"<<no;
                cout<<"\nName:"<<name;
                cout<<"\nTotal:"<<total;
                float per=total/5;
                cout<<"\nPercentage:"<<per;
        }
};
int main( )
```

```
{
        stud s;
        s.get_data( );
        s.put_data( );
        return 0;
}
```

2) Outside the class definition:

- Another method of function declaration is we just declare function inside a class and define it separately outside a class.
- A function define outside a class contains a membership 'identity label' in the header which tells the compiler which class the function belongs to.
- The membership label **class-name ::** tells the compiler the function *function-name* belongs to the class *class-name*. The scope of function is restricted to the *class-name* specified in the header line. The symbol **::** is called ***scope resolution operator.***

Syntax:

```
return-type class-name :: function-name(argument
declaration)
{
    Function body
}
```

For example :

```
class stud
{
     //by default private
       int no;
       char name[20];
       int total;
     public:
       void get_data();
       void put_data();
} ;

void stud::get_data()
{
        cout<<"\n\n\nEnter No:";
        cin>>no;
        cout<<"\nEnter Name:";
        cin>>name;
        cout<<"\nEnter Total:";
        cin>>total;
}
```

```
void stud::put_data()
{
        cout<<"\n\n\nNo:"<<no;
        cout<<"\nName:"<<name;
        cout<<"\nTotal:"<<total;
        float per=total/5;
        cout<<"\nPercentage:"<<per;
}
int main( )
{
        stud s;
        s.get_data( );
        s.put_data( );
        return 0;
}
```

Special characteristics of member function:

- Several different classes can use same function name. The 'membership label' will resolve their scope.
- Member function can access the private data of the class. A non-member function cannot do so. (However, an exception to this rule is a **friend function.**)
- A member function can call another member function directly, without using a dot (.) operator.

Making an outside function inline:

- To separate the details of implementations from the class definition is one of the objectives of OOP. For example, to declare function inside a class and define it outside a class is one of the objectives of OOP.
- It is there for good practice to define the member functions outside the calss.
- To make a function **inline** just use the qualifier **inline** in the header line of function definition.
- Member functions that are defined within a class are inline by default.

  Syntax :

  ```
  inline return-type class-name :: function-name(argument declaration)
  {
          Function body
  }
  ```

For example :

```
class stud
{
  //by default private
        int no;
        char name[20];
```

```
        int total;
    public:
        void get_data()
        {
                cout<<"\n\n\nEnter No:";
                cin>>no;
                cout<<"\nEnter Name:";
                cin>>name;
                cout<<"\nEnter Total:";
                cin>>total;
        }
        void put_data();
};

        inline void stud::put_data()  //defining outside function
inline
        {
                cout<<"\n\n\nNo:"<<no;
                cout<<"\nName:"<<name;
                 cout<<"\nTotal:"<<total;
                float per=total/5;
                cout<<"\nPercentage:"<<per;
        }
        int main( )
        {
                stud s;
                s.get_data( );
                s.put_data( );
                return 0;
        }
```

Nesting of member Function :

- To call a member function by using its name inside another member function of same class is known as nesting of member function.

  For Example :

```
class stud
{
        //by default private
        int no,total,age;
        char name[20],address[40],bdate[10];
        public:
        void get_data()
        {
                cout<<"\n\n\nEnter No:";
                cin>>no;
                cout<<"\nEnter Name:";
                cin>>name;
```

```
            get_personal_data(); //Nesting of member function
            cout<<"\nEnter Total:";
            cin>>total;
        }
         void get_personal_data()
        {
            cout<<"\nEnter age:";
            cin>>age;
            cout<<"\nEnter address:";
            cin>>address;
            cout<<"\nEnter Birth date:";
            cin>>bdate;
        }
        void put_personal_data()
        {
            cout<<"Age:"<<age;
            cout<<"\nAddress:"<<address;
            cout<<"\nBirth date:"<<bdate;
        }
        void put_data();
} s1;
        inline void stud::put_data()
        {
            cout<<"\n\n\nNo:"<<no;
            cout<<"\nName:"<<name;
            put_personal_data(); //Nesting of member function
            cout<<"\nTotal:"<<total;
            float per=total/5;
            cout<<"\nPercentage:"<<per;
        }
int main( )
{
        s1.get_data( );
        s1.put_data( );
        return 0;
}
```

Private Member Function:

- A private member function can only be called by another function that is a member of its class.
- Even an object cannot invoke a private function using a dot operator.
- Normally, when we want to hide some information from outside or want to restrict the control at that time we declare such a function as a private function. Like incrementing salary of employee, personal information of students.

For example :

```
#include<conio.h>
#include<iostream.h>
class test
{
        int cpp,vb,php;
        void read();  //private member function
  public:
        void update();
        void print();
};
void test::read()
{
        cout<<"\nEnter marks of cpp:";
        cin>>cpp;
        cout<<"\nEnter marks of vb:";
        cin>>vb;
        cout<<"\nEnter marks of php";
        cin>>php;
}
void test::print()
{
        cout<<"\n\nMarks of cpp:"<<cpp;
        cout<<"\nMarks of vb:"<<vb;
        cout<<"\nMarks of php"<<php;
}
void test::update()
{
        read();
}
void main()
{
        test t;
        clrscr();
         //t.read();    //not accessible as private function
        t.update();
        t.print();
        getch()
}
```

Memory allocation for objects:

- We have stated that the memory space for objects is allocated when they are declared and not when the class is specified. This statement is only partly true.
- Actually, the member function are created and placed in the memory space only when they are defined as a part of a class specification.

- All the objects belonging to that class use the same member function. No separate space is allocated for member function when the objects are created.
- Only the space for member variables is allocated separately for each object.
- Separate memory locations for each object are essential, because the member variables will hold different data values for different objects.

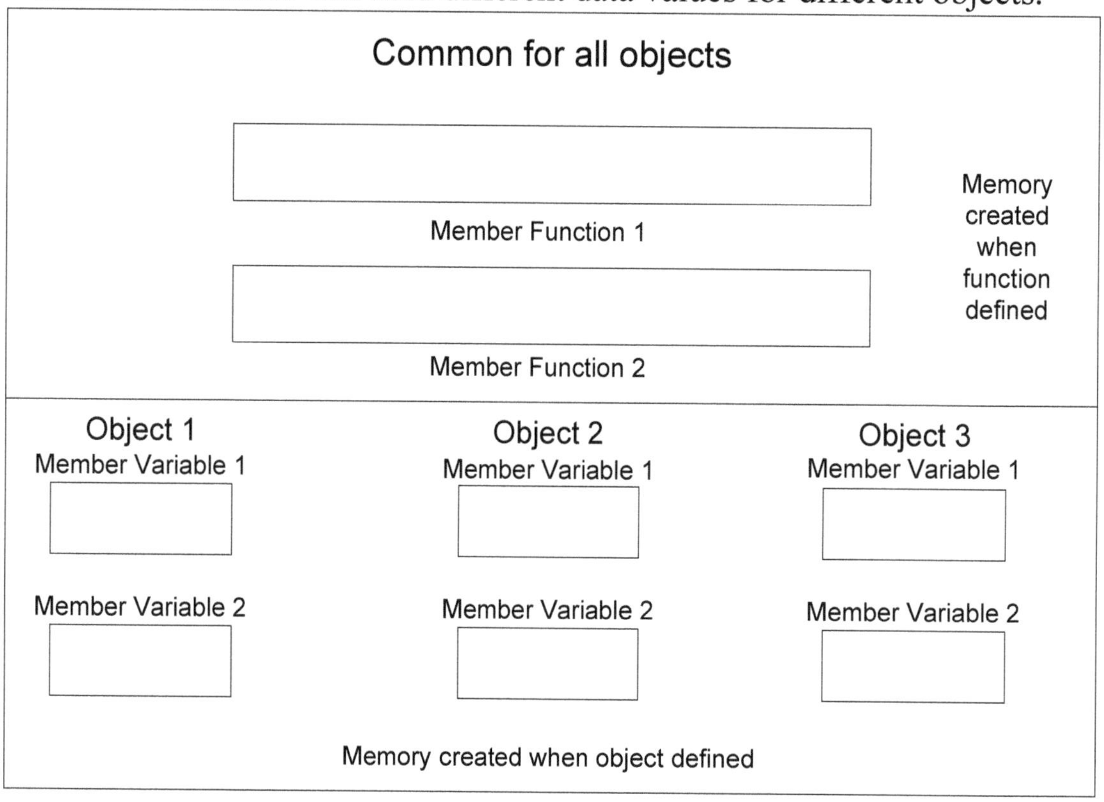

For Example:

```
#include<iostream.h>
#include<conio.h>
class temp
{
        int a;
        char b;
        float c;
  public:
        void get(int x, char y, float z)
        {
                a = x;
                b = y;
                c = z;
        }
        void put()
        {
                cout<<a<<b<<c;
        }
```

```
};
//No memory allocation is done when class is specified.

int main()
{
        temp t1, t2; //Memory allocation done when object declared
        clrscr();
        t1.get(10, 'a', 10.20);
        t2.get(20, 'b', 20.20);
        cout<<"\nSize of t1:"<<sizeof(t1);
        cout<<"\nSize of t2:"<<sizeof(t2);
        return 0;
}
```

Output:

```
Size of t1:7
Size of t2:7
```

Static Data Members or Static Class variables:

What is a static data member?

- Class members can be declared using the storage class specifier static in the class member list. Only one copy of the static member is shared by all objects of a class in a program.
- When you declare an object of a class having a static member, the static member is not part of the class object.

Characteristics of static data members (member variables) are:

- It is initialized to 0 (zero) when the first object of its class is created.
- Only one copy of that member is created for the entire class and is shared by all objects of that class, no matter how many objects are created.
- It is visible only within a class, but its lifetime is entire program.

Use of static data member :

- A typical use of static members is for recording data common to all objects of a class.
- For example, you can use a static data member as a counter to store the number of objects of a particular class type that are created. Each time a new object is created, this static data member can be incremented to keep track of the total number of objects.
- In sort static variables are normally used to maintain values common to entire class.

  Example:

```
#include <conio.h>
#include <iostream.h>
class item
{
    static int count;
    int number;
```

```
    public :
    void getdata(int a)
    {
            number = a;
            count ++;
    }
    void getcount(void)
    {
            cout<<"\n Count :"<<count;
    }
};
int item :: count;          // definition of static data member
int main( )
{
    item a, b, c;           //count is initialized to zero
    a.getcount( );                  //display count
    b.getcount( );
    c.getcount( );

    a.getdata(100);         //getting data into object a
    b.getdata(200);         //getting data into object b
    c.gatdata(300 );        //getting data into object c

    count<<"\n After reading data:"
    a.getcount( );                  //display count
    b.getcount( );
    c.getcount( );
    return 0;
}
```

Note:

- Notice the following statement in the program :
  int item :: count *// definition of static data member*
- Note that the type and scope of each static member variable must be defined outside the class definition. This is necessary because the static data members are stored separately rather than as a part of an object. Since they are associated with the class itself rather than with any class object, they are also known as class variables.
- Static variables are like non-inline member function as they are declared in a class declaration and defined in the source file.
- While defining a static variable, some initial value can also be assigned to the variable. For instance, the following definition gives count the initial value 10.

int item :: count = 10;

Static Member Function:

- A static function can have access to only other static members (function or variable) declared in the same class.
- A static member function can be called using the class name(instead of its objects) like this:

  class-name :: function-name;

  Example:

```
#include<iostream.h>
#include<conio.h>
#include<string.h>
class stud
{
    static int count_stud;
    int no;
    char name[20];
   public:
    void get_data(char s_name[])
    {
          count_stud++;
          no=count_stud;
          strcpy(name,s_name);
    }
    static void get_stud_count()     //defining static member function
    {
          cout<<"\nTotal students are :"<<count_stud;
    }
    void display()
    {
          cout<<"\n\tNo:"<<no<<"\tName:"<<name;
    }
};

int stud::count_stud;                    //by default 0

int main()
{
 stud s1,s2,s3;
 clrscr();
 s1.get_stud_count();
 s2.get_stud_count();
 s3.get_stud_count();

 s1.get_data("Asha");
 s2.get_data("Nisha");
 s3.get_data("Mina");
 cout<<"\nAfter entering data:";
```

```
  stud::get_stud_count();              //accessing static member function

  cout<<"\n\n\n\tstudents Info\n\n";
  s1.display();
  s2.display();
  s3.display();
  return 0;
}
```

Output:

Total students are :0
Total students are :0
Total students are :0
After entering data:
Total students are :3
students Info
No:1 Name:Asha
No:2 Name:Nisha
No:3 Name:Mina

Array of objects:

- Array of variables that are of type class are called array of objects.

  Example:

```
#include<conio.h>
#include<iostream.h>
const n=3;
class item
{
        int no;
        char name[20];
        char company[20];
        int qty;
public:
        void get_data(int );
        void display();
};
void item::get_data(int i_no)
{
        no=i_no;
        cout<<"\n\n\nEnter Item name:";
        cin>>name;
        cout<<"\nEnter Item Company:";
        cin>>company;
        cout<<"\nEnter Qty:";
        cin>>qty;
}
int main()
```

```
{
        clrscr();
        item t[n];
        for(int i=0; i<n; i++)
        {
                t[i].get_data(i+1);
        }
        for(i=0; i<n; i++)
        {
                t[i].display();
        }
    return 0;
}
void item::display()
{
        cout<<"\n\n\nItem No:\t"<<no;
        cout<<"\nItem name:\t"<<name;
        cout<<"\nItem Company:\t"<<company;
        cout<<"\nQty:\t"<<qty;
}
```

Output:

```
Enter Item name:monitor
Enter Item Company:lg
Enter Qty:1

Enter Item name:speaker
Enter Item Company:creative
Enter Qty:2

Enter Item name:mouse
Enter Item Company:HP
Enter Qty:1

Item No:        1
Item name:      monitor
Item Company:   lg
Qty:    1

Item No:        2
Item name:      speaker
Item Company:   creative
Qty:    2

Item No:        3
Item name:      mouse
Item Company:   HP
```

Qty: 1

Object as Function Argument:

- Like any other data type an object may be used as a function argument. This can be done in two ways.
  1) A copy of entire object is passed to the function ***(Pass by value).***
  2) Only the address of the object is transferred to the function ***(Pass by reference)***.

  (1) Pass by value:

  In this method a copy of entire object is passed to the function. As the copy of object is passed to the function any changes made to this object inside a function do not affect the object used to call the function.

  (2) Pass by reference:

  In this method only the address of the object is transferred to the function. When an address of the object is passed to the called function works directly on the actual object used in the call. Means any changes made to the object inside the function will reflect in the actual object. This method is more efficient since it requires passing only an address of the object and not entire object.

  Example:

```
# include <iostream.h>
# include <conio.h>
class time
{
        int hours;
        int minutes;
       public:
        void gettime(int h, int m)
        {
                hours = h;
                minutes = m;
        }
        void puttime(void)
        {
                cout << hours << "Hours and ";
                cout << minutes << "Minutes " << "\n";
        }
        void sum(time, time);
};
void time :: sum(time t1, time t2)
{
        minutes = t1.minutes + t2.minutes ;
        hours = minutes / 60;
        minutes = minutes % 60;
        hours = hours + t1.hours + t2.hours ;
```

```
}

int main( )
{
        time t1, t2, t3;
        t1.gettime(2, 45);
        t2.gettime(3, 30) ;
        t3.sum(t1, t2);
        cout << "T1 = "; t1.puttime( );        //display t1
        cout << "T2 = " ; t2.puttime( );       //display t2
        cout <<"T3 = "; t3.puttime( );         //display t3
        return 0 ;
}
```

Friend Function:

- We know that the private members cannot be accessed from outside the class. That is, a non-member function cannot have an access to the private data of a calss.
- A friend function is used for accessing the non-public members of a class. A class can allow non-member functions and other classes to access its own private data, by making them friends. Thus, a friend function is an ordinary function or a member of another class. Such a function need not be a member for any of these classes.
- To make an outside function 'friendly' to a class, simply declare this function as a friend of class like this :

```
class abc
{
        .......
        .......
  public:
        friend void xyz();      //friend function declaration
};
```

- The friend function can be defined elsewhere in a program like normal c++ function.
- The function can be declared as a friend in any number of classes.
- A friend function has full access rights to the private member of a class.
- It can be declared either public or private part of a class without affecting its meaning.
- Cases of using a friend function:
    (1) One simple normal function is a friend of one class.
    (2) One simple normal function is a friend of more than one class.
    (3) A member function of one class is a friend of another class.
    (4) One class is a friend of another class.

Characteristics of friend function:

- It is not in the scope of the class to which it has been declared as friend.
- Since it is not in the scope of the class, it cannot be called using the object of that class.
- It can be invoked (called) like a normal function without the help of any object.
- Unlike member function, it cannot access the member names directly and has to use an object name and dot membership operator with each member name.
- It can be declared either in the public or the private part of a class without affecting its meaning.
- Usually, it has the objects as arguments.

Note : ***The friend function are often used in operator overloading.***

- **Example of one simple normal function is a friend of one class:**

```
#include<conio.h>
#include<iostream.h>
class temp
{
        int a;
        int b;
      public:
        void getdata(int x,int y)
        {
                a=x;
                b=y;
        }
        friend int sum(temp);
};
int sum(temp t)
{
         return t.a+t.b;
}
int main()
{
        temp t;
        clrscr();
        t.getdata(10, 20);
         int s = sum(t);
        cout<<"\nSum is:"<<s;
        getch();
        return 0;
}
```

Output:

Sum is : 30

Note: *The friend function accesses the class variables **a** and **b** by using the dot operator and the object passed to it. The function call **sum(t)** passes the object t by value to the friend function.*

- Member function of one class can be friend function of another class. In such cases, they are defined the scope resolution operator which is shown as follow :

```
class X
{
        ........
        int fun1( ) ;
        .......
};
class Y
{
        ...............
        friend int X :: fun1( ) ;            //fun1() of class X
                                             // is friend of class Y
        ..................
};
```

- The function **fun1** is a member of **class X** and friend of **class Y**

➢ **Example of a member function of one class is a friend of another class:**

```
#include<conio.h>
#include<iostream.h>
class value;          //forward declaration
class max
{
        public:
        int max_val(value v);
};
class value
{
        int val1, val2;
        public:
        friend int max::max_val(value v);
        void get(int x, int y)
        {
                val1 = x;
                val2=y;
        }
};
int max::max_val(value v)
{
```

```
        return v.val1 > v.val2 ? v.val1 : v.val2;
}
int main()
{
        value x;
        clrscr();
        x.get(10, 20);
        max m;
        cout<<"\nMax:"<<m.max_val(x);
        getch();
        return 0;
}
```

- We can also declare all the member functions of one class as the friend functions of another class. In such cases, the class is called a friend class. This can be specified as follow:

```
        class Z
        {
                friend class X;    //all member functions of class X are friends to Z
        };
```

- **Example of one class is a friend of another class:**

```
#include<conio.h>
#include<iostream.h>
class max;          //forward declaration
class value
{
        int val1, val2;
        friend class max;
                public:
        void get(int x, int y)
        {
                val1 = x;
                val2 = y;
        }
};

class max
{
        public:
        int max_val(value v);
};

int max::max_val(value v)
{
        return v.val1 > v.val2 ? v.val1 : v.val2;
```

```
}

int main()
{
        value x;
        clrscr();
        x.get(10,20);
        max m;
        cout<<"\nMax:"<<m.max_val(x);
        getch();
        return 0;
}
```

Output:

Max:20

Function Returning object:

Functions can also return objects.

Example:

```
#include<conio.h>
#include<iostream.h>
class exp
{
        int x;
        int y;
        public:
        void get(int a, int b)
        {
                x = a;
                y = b;
        }
        void print()
        {
                cout<<"\n"<<x<<"x + "<<y<<"y";
        }
        friend exp sum(exp e1,exp e2);
};
exp sum(exp e1,exp e2)
{
        exp e;
        e.x=e1.x+e2.x;
        e.y=e1.y+e2.y;
        return e;
}
int main()
```

```
{
        exp e1,e2,e;
        clrscr();
        e1.get(10,20);
        e2.get(5,10);
        e1.print();
        e2.print();
        cout<<"\n----------------";
        e=sum(e1,e2);
        e.print();
        getch();
        return 0;
}
```

Output:

```
        10x + 20y
        5x + 10y
        ----------------
        15x + 30y
```

Const member function:

- A const member function cannot change a value of data member of a class. (But it can change value of static data member of a class.)
- To make a member function constant we have to use 'const' keyword at both following places-
  1) **At the declaration of member function.**
  2) **At the definition of member function.**

  Example

```
    #include<conio.h>
    #include<iostream.h>
    int i=0;
    class stud
    {
            static int cnt;
            int no;
            char name[20];
     public:
            void get()
            {
                    cout<<"\nEnter no:";
                    cin>>no;
                    cout<<"\nEnter name:";
                    cin>>name;
            }
            void put() const; //constants function
```

```
};
int stud::cnt;
void stud :: put() const        // constatnt function
{
    // cout<<"\nEnter no:";
    // cin>>no                       // This statement will not change
value of no.

    cout<<"\nNo:"<<no;
    cout<<"\nName:"<<name;

    cnt++;              // You can change value of cnt as it is static
data member
    i++;                //You can change value of i as it is global
variable.
    cout<<"\n cnt:"<<cnt;
    cout<<"\n i:"<<i;
  }
int main()
{
    clrscr();
    stud s;
    s.get();
    s.put();
    getch();
    return 0;
}
```

Pointer to member:

- C++ permits us to access the class members through pointers. In order to achieve this, C++ provides a set of three pointers to member operators. They are also known as member dereferencing operators.

Member dereferencing operators :

(1) ::* To declare a pointer to a member of a class.

```
class temp
{
   public:
       int  x, y;
       void get();
};
int temp::*xx;       //Pointer of a data member
xx= &temp::x;
```

- Here, temp ::* means pointer to a member of a class temp.

(2) .* To access a member using a pointer to the object and pointer to that member.

```
temp t1;
int  temp ::* xx;
xx=&temp::x;
cout<<"\nX="<<t1.*xx;
```

(3) →* To access a member using a pointer to the object and pointer to that member.

```
temp t1;
temp *t;
t=&t1;  //Pointer of object

int temp::*xx;
xx=&temp::x;
cout<<"\nX:"<<t→*xx;
```

Pointer to a member function:

- We can also design pointer to a member function. It is known as call back function.
  (object-name .* pointer to member function) ();
  (pointer to object →* pointer to member function) ();
  <u>**Note:**</u>
  The precedence of () is higher than that of . and →*, so the parentheses are necessary.*
  Example:

```
#include<conio.h>
#include<iostream.h>
class temp
{
        public:
        int x;
        int y;
        void get(int a,int b)
        {
                x=a;
                y=b;
        }
        int sum()
        {
                return x+y;
        }
        void display()
        {
```

```
                cout<<"\n\n\nX:="<<x;
                cout<<"\nY:="<<y;
        }
};
int main()
{
        clrscr();
         temp t1;
        temp *t;
        t=&t1;//pointer of object
        cout<<"\n\nPointer of object";
        t->get(10,20);
        t->display();
        int temp::*xx;//pointer of data member
        xx=&temp::x;
        int temp::*yy;
        yy=&temp::y;
        cout<<"\n\nPointer of data member";
        cout<<"\nX:="<<t1.*xx;//or t1.x;
        cout<<"\ny:="<<t1.*yy;
        t1.*xx=100;// or t1.x=100;
        cout<<"\nX:="<<t->*xx;

        void (temp::*d)();//pointer to member function
        d=&temp::display;
        cout<<"\n\nPointer of data function";
        (t1.*d)();
        int (temp::*s)();
        s=&temp::sum;
        cout<<"\nSum:="<<(t->*s)();
        getch();
        return 0;
}
```

Output:

```
Pointer of object
X:=10
Y:=20

Pointer of data member
X:=10
y:=20
X:=100

Pointer of data function
X:=100
```

Y:=20
Sum:=120

UNIT-5
Constructor and Destructor

5.1 What is constructor?

- A constructor is a 'special' member function whose task is to initialize the object of its class.
- Constructor name is the same as the class name.
- Constructor is invoked whenever an object of its associated class is created.
- It is called constructor because it construct the value of data members of a class.

Why constructor is required?

- Up till now to assign value to private member of a class we have used member methods.
- To invoke these member methods we first required object of a class to be created and with the help of this object we invoke member methods to assign value to private data members.
- To solve this problem C++ provides a special member function called the constructor which enables an object to initialize itself when it is created. This is known as "*automatic initialization*" of object.

Characteristic of Constructor:

1) They should be declared in the public section.
2) They are invoked automatically when the object are created.
3) They do not have return types, not even void and therefore, they cannot return values.
4) They cannot be inherited, though a derived class can call the base class constructor.
5) Like other C++ functions, they can have default arguments.
6) Constructor cannot be virtual.
7) We cannot refer to their address.
8) An object with a constructor (or destructor) cannot be used as a member of union.
9) They make 'implicit calls' to the operator **new** and **delete** when memory allocation is required.

Note:

If there is no constructor exists for the class and one is needed, the compiler implicitly declares a default (parameter less) constructor. This constructor is an inline public member of its class. (Same for destructor.)

Different types of constructors:

1) ***Default constructor***
2) ***Parameterized constructor***

3) ***Multiple constructor***
4) ***Copy constructor***
5) ***Constructor with default arguments***

(1) Default constructor :

- A constructor can take zero or more arguments.
- "A constructor with zero arguments (that is no arguments) is known as default constructor."

Example:

```
#include<conio.h>
#include<iostream.h>
class temp
{
      int x,y;
  public:
    temp()
      {
          x=0;
          y=0;
      }
      void put()
      {
          cout<<"\n\n\nX:"<<x;
          cout<<"\nY:"<<y;
      }
};
int main()
{
      clrscr();
      temp t;
      t.put();
      getch();
      return 0;
}
```

(2) Parameterized constructor :

- *"A constructor that can take arguments is called parameterized constructor."*
- If we want to initialize all data members of objects with different value at the time of creation we can use parameterized constructor.
- We can pass the initial values as arguments to the constructor function when an object is created in two ways:

(1) By calling constructor implicitly.

temp t(100,200);   ***//Implicit call***

(2) By calling constructor explicitly.

temp t1=temp(100,200);   ***//Explicit call***

Example:

```
#include<conio.h>
#include<iostream.h>
class temp
```

```
{
    int x;
    int y;
 public:
    temp(int a,int b)
    {
         x=a;
         y=b;
    }
  void put()
    {
         cout<<"\n\n\nX:"<<x;
         cout<<"\nY:"<<y;
    }
};
int main()
{
    clrscr();
    temp t(100,200);         //implicit call
    t.put();
    temp t1=temp(10,20);   //explicit call
    t1.put();
    getch();
    return 0;
}
```

(3) Multiple constructors :

When more than one constructor is used in a single class it is called multiple constructors.

Example:

```
#include<conio.h>
#include<iostream.h>

class temp
{
        int x;
        int y;

    public:
        temp()
        {
            x=10;
            y=20;
        }
        temp(int a, int b);              // Declaration of
constructor
        void put()
```

```
        {
            cout<<"\n\n\nX:"<<x;
            cout<<"\nY:"<<y;
        }
} t3(11,12);        //globle variable

temp::temp(int a, int b)        //Defination of constructor
{
    x=a;
    y=b;
}
int main()
{
    clrscr();
    temp t1(100,200);
    t1.put();

    temp t2;
    t2.put();

    t3.put();
    getch();
    return 0;
}
```

(4) Copy constructor :

- A copy constructor is used to declare and initialize an object form another object.
- The process of initializing through a copy constructor is known as copy initialization.
- A reference variable has been used as an argument to the copy constructor. We cannot pass the argument by value to a copy constructor.

Note:

When no copy constructor is defined, the compiler supplies its own copy constructor.

Example:

```
#include<conio.h>
#include<iostream.h>
class copy
{
    int x, y;
  public:
    copy(int a,int b)
    {
```

```
                x=a;
                y=b;
        }
        copy(copy &t)
        {
                x=t.x;
        }
        void put()
        {
           cout<<"\n\nX:"<<x;
           cout<<"\nY:"<<y;
        }
};
int main()
{
        clrscr();
        copy t1(100,200);
        t1.put();
        copy t2(t1);            //copy constructor
        t2.put();
  getch();
  return 0;
}
```

(5) Constructor with default arguments:

It is possible to define constructor with default arguments.

Example:

```
#include<conio.h>
#include<iostream.h>
class temp
{
        int x;
        int y;
     public:
        temp (int a=1, int b=2);
        void put()
        {
                cout<<"\n\n\nX:"<<x;
                cout<<"\nY:"<<y;
        }
};
temp::temp(int a,int b)
{
        x=a;
        y=b;
}
int main()
```

```
{
        clrscr();
        int a=100, b=200;
        temp t1(a,b);
        t1.put();
        temp t2;
        t2.put();
        temp t3(a);
        t3.put();
getch();
return 0;
}
```

5.2 Dynamic initialization of object :

- Class objects can be initialized dynamically. You may provide initial value of an object during run time. So advantage of dynamic initialization is that you can provide different format of data at run time depending upon the situation.

Example:

```
#include<conio.h>
#include<iostream.h>
class interest
{
        int p,n,r;
       public:
        interest()
        {
        }

        interest(int amt,int year,int rate)
        {
                p=amt;
                n=year;
                r=rate;
        }
        void si_int()
        {
                cout<<"\nSimple Interest:"<<(p*r*n)/100;
        }
};
int main()
{
        clrscr();
        int p,r,n;
        cout<<"Enter amount,rate and no. of years:";
        cin>>p>>r>>n;
        interest i;
```

```
        i=interest(p,n,r);
        i.si_int();
        getch();
        return 0;
}
```

5.3 Destructor:

- Destructor destroys the objects when they are no longer required.
- It is used to destroy the objects that have been created by constructor.
- Destructor member function name is the same as the class name but preceded by the **tiled(~)** sign.

  Example :

```
class temp
{
        .....
        public:
        .....
        ~temp()
        {
                .....
        }
};
```

- It never takes any argument nor does it return any value.
- It will be invoked (called) by compiler upon exit from the program to clean up the storage that is no longer accessible.
- Destructors are called in reverse of order of object creation.

Why destructor?

- Local objects (objects which are created in main or in any function) are created when their block is entered and destroyed when the block is left. Global object are destroyed when the program terminates.
- Object may require deleting memory that it has previously allocated. But it happens normally only when it goes out of scope. In C++ we can handle this with destructor.
- C++ provides a function called destructor that destroys the objects when they are no longer required.

  Example:

```
#include<conio.h>
#include<iostream.h>
class temp
{
                int no;
                int x;
                int y;
        public:
```

```
                temp(int n)
                {
                x=10;
                y=20;
                no=n;
                }
                void put()
                {
                cout<<"\nX:"<<x;
                cout<<"\nY:"<<y;
                }
                ~temp()             //Destructor
                {
                cout<<"\ndelete "<<no;
                }
} t(1);


int main()
{
        clrscr();
        temp c(2);
        c.put();
        t.put();
        getch();
        return 0;
}
```

Dynamic Constructor:

- ***Allocation of memory to object at the time of their construction is known as dynamic construction of object.***
- The constructor can also be used to allocate memory while creating object. This will enable the system to allocate right amount of memory for each object when object are not of the same size, thus resulting in the saving of memory.
- The memory is allocated with the help of new operator.

  Example:

```
#include<conio.h>
#include<iostream.h>
#include<string.h>
class dynamic
{
        char *name;
        int len;
```

```
public:
  dynamic(char *s)
  {
        len=strlen(s);
        name=new char[len+1];
        strcpy(name,s);
  }
  ~dynamic()
  {
        delete name;
        cout<<"del";
  }
  void display()
  {
        cout<<endl<<len<<endl<<name;
  }
};



int main()
{
      clrscr();
      dynamic d("Atmiya");
      dynamic d1("bhulku");
      d.display();
      d1.display();
      getch();
      return 0;
}
```

Constructing two dimensional arrays:

We can construct matrix variable using the class type objects. The example illustrates how to construct a matrix of size m x n;

Example:

```
#include<conio.h>
#include<iostream.h>
class matrix
{
   int **p;
   int row,col;
 public:
   matrix(int r,int c);
   void get(int i,int j,int val)
   {
         p[i][j]=val;
```

```
    }
    int put(int i,int j)
    {
        return p[i][j];
    }
    ~matrix()
    {
        delete p;
        cout<<"del";
    }
};

    matrix::matrix(int r,int c)
    {
        row=r;
        col=c;
        p=new int *[row];

        for(int i=0;i<row;i++)
        {
            p[i]=new int[col];
        }
    }
    int main()
    {
        clrscr();
        int row,col;
        cout<<"\nEnter size of matrix";
        cin>>row>>col;

        matrix m(row,col);
        int val;
        for(int i=0;i<row;i++)
        {
            for(int j=0;j<col;j++)
            {
                cout<<"Enter value of m["<<i<<"]["<<j<<"]=";
                cin>>val;
                m.get(i,j,val);
            }
        }
        cout<<"\n\n"<<row<<"*"<<col<<" matrix:\n\n";
        for(i=0;i<row;i++)
        {
            cout<<endl;
            for(int j=0;j<col;j++)
```

```
            {
                cout<<"\t"<<m.put(i,j);
            }
        }
    return 0;
    }
```

The constructor first creates a vector pointer to an **int** of size **row**. Then, it allocates, iteratively an **int** type vector of size **col** pointed at by each element **p[i]**. Thus, space for the elements of a **row x col** matrix is allocated from free store as shown below:

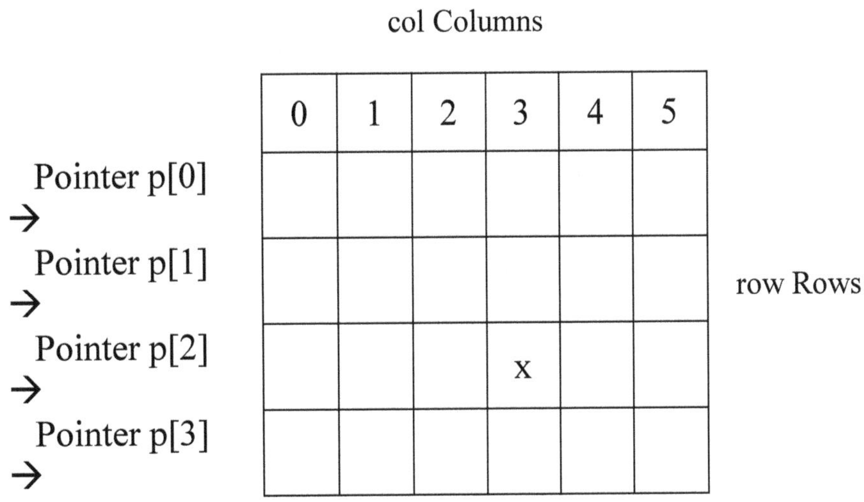

x represent the element p[2][3]

Unit - 6

Operator Overloading and Type Conversions

6.1 Introduction:

⇒ Operator overloading is one of the many exciting features of C++ language. It is an important technique that enhanced the power of extensibility of C++.

⇒ C++ tries to make the user-defined data types behave in much the same as the built-in types. For instance, C++ permits us to add two variables of user-defines types with the basic types.

⇒ This means that C++ has the ability to provide the operators with a special meaning for a data type. The mechanism of giving such special meanings to an operator is known as **operator overloading**.

⇒ Operator overloading provides a flexible option for the creation of new definitions for most of the C++ operators. We can overload (give additional meaning to) all the C++ operators except the following:

- ***Class member access operators (. , .*).***
- ***Scope resolution operator (::).***
- ***Size operator (sizeof).***
- ***Conditional operator (? :).***

⇒ Although the semantics of an operator can be extended, we cannot change its syntax, the grammatical rules that govern its use such as the number of operands, precedence and associativity.

Defining Operator Overloading:-

⇒ To define an additional task to an operator, we must specify what it means in relation to the class to which the operator is applied. This is done with the help of a special function, called **operator function**, which describes the task.

⇒ The general form of an operator function is:

```
return type classname :: operator op (arglist)
{
    Function body     //task defines
}
```

Where ***return type*** is the type of value returned by the specified operation and ***op*** is the operator being overloaded. The ***op*** is preceded by the keyword operator. **operator *op*** is the function name.

⇒ Operator function must be either member functions (non-static) or friend functions. A basic difference between them is that a friend function will have only one argument for unary operators and two for binary operators, while a member function has no arguments for unary operators and only one for binary operators.

⇒ This is because the object used to invoke the member function is passed implicitly and therefore is available for the member function. This is not the case with friend functions. Arguments may be passed either by value or by reference.

⇒ The process of overloading involves the following steps:

1. Create a class that defines the data type that is to be used in the overloading operation.
2. Declare the operator function **operator *op* ()** in the public part of the class. It may be either a member function or a friend function.
3. Defines the operator function to implement the required operations.

⇒ Overloaded operator functions can be invoked by expressions such as

op* x** or **x *op for unary operators and

x *op* y for binary operators.

⇒ op x (or x op) would be interpreted as operator op(x) for friend functions. Similarly, the expression x op y would be interpreted as either x.operator op (v) in case of member functions, or operator op (x,y) in case of friend functions.

Overloading Unary Operators:-

⇒ Unary operator takes only one operand for example unary minus operator. It changes the sign of an operand when applied to a basic type.

⇒ The following program shows the unary minus operator is overloaded as a member function of the class.

```
#include<iostream.h>
#include<conio.h>
Class point
{
        private:
                int x;
                int y;
        public:
                void getdata( )
                {
                        cout<<"\n enter x:";
                        cin >> x ;
                        cout<<"\n enter y:";
                        cin>>y;
                }

                void putdata( )
                {
                        cout<<"\n ( "<< x <<" , "<<y <<" )";
                }
                point operator – ()
                {
```

```
                point temp;
                temp.x=-x;
                temp.y=-y;
                return temp;
            }
};
int main()
{
        point p1,p2;
        p1.getdata();

        p2= -p1;

        p1.putdata();
        p2.putdata();
        return 0;
}
```

⇒ Here, we have implemented operator –() function as a member of class point.

⇒ Now, the statement p2= - p1; will make a call to this function as p2= p1.operator –();

⇒ P1 object is invoked implicitly in the function. The function will change the sign of the data members of the objects using temp.x= -x and temp.y= -y statements.

⇒ In temp.x= -x statement, -x is the member variable x of the object p1, because the function is called using the object p1.

Overloading Binary Operator:-

⇒ Binary operator will have two operands to perform operation. So, we have to pass one external argument to our member function that overloads the binary operator.

⇒ The following example show an example of overloading + operator

Example :

```
#include<iostream.h>
Class point
{
  private:
        int x;
        int y;
  public:
        point()
        {
                x=y=0;
        }
        void getdata( )
```

```
        {
                cout<<"\n enter x:";
                cin >> x ;
                cout<<"\n enter y:";
                cin>>y;
        }
        void putdata( )
        {
                Cout<<"\n ( "<< x <<" , "<<y <<" )";
        }
        point operator + (point p)
        {
                point temp;
                Temp.x=x+p.x;
                Temp.y=y+p.y;
                return temp;
        }
};
int main()
{
        point p1,p2;
        p1.getdata();
        p2.getdata();
        point p3;
        p3=p1+p2;
        p1.putdata();
        p2.putdata();
        p3.putdata();
        return 0;
}
```

In this example we have overloaded operator+ () function, we should note the following features of this function:

1. It receives only one point type argument explicitly.
2. It returns a point type value.
3. It is a member function of point.

The statement **p3=p1+p2** is equivalent to **p3= p1.operator+ (p2);**
As a rule, in overloading of binary operators, the left-hand operand is used to invoke the operator function and the right-hand operand is passed as an argument.

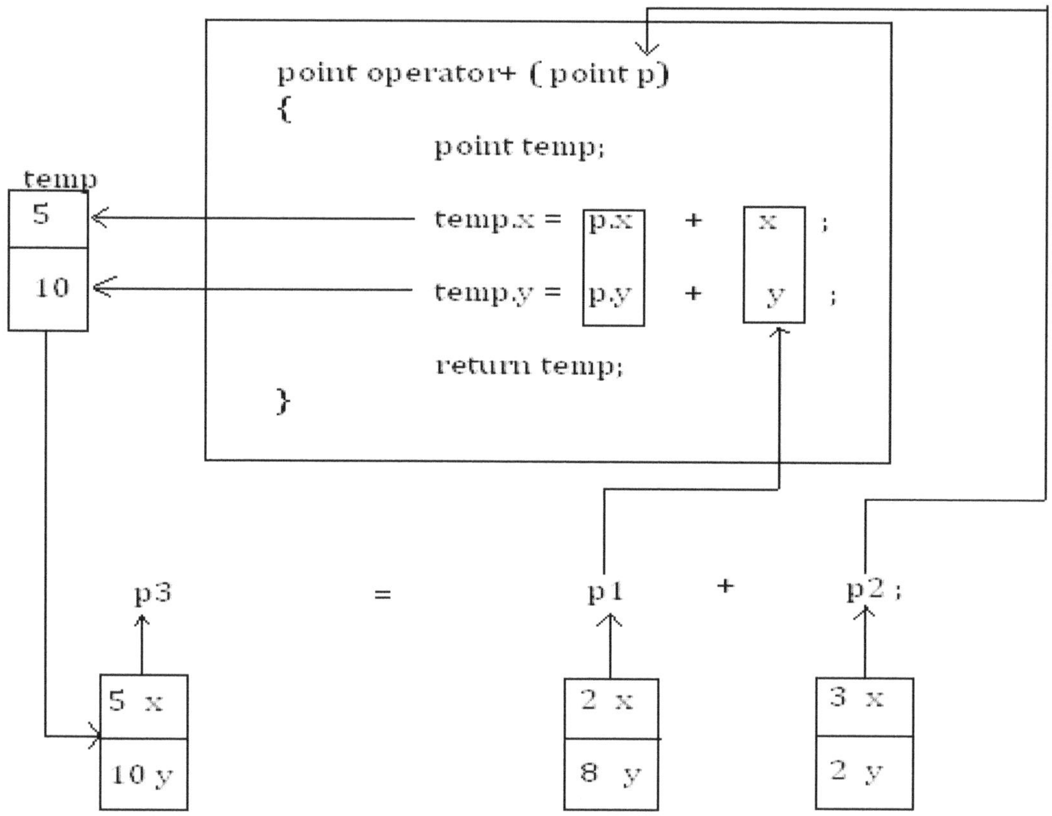

Implementation of the overloaded + operator

Overloading Binary Operators Using Friends:-

⇒ Friend functions may be used in the place of member functions for overloading a binary operator, the only difference being that a friend function requires two arguments to be explicitly passed to it, while a member functions require only one.

⇒ In the program of point class, we have to modify the following statements.

1. Replace the member function declaration by the friend function declaration.
   Friend point operator + (point, point);
2. Redefine the operator function as follows:

```
point operator+( point a, point b)
{
    point temp;
    temp.x = a.x + b.y;
    temp.y = a.y + b.y;
    return temp;
}
```

In this case, the statement **p3 = p1 + p2;** is equivalent to
c3 = operator+(p1,p2);

Example:

```
#include<iostream.h>
class point
{
```

```
    private:
        int x;
        int y;
    public:
        point()
        {
                x=y=0;
        }
        friend point operator + (point , point);
        friend istream & operator>> (istream&, point &);
        friend ostream & operator<< ( ostream &, point &);
};
point operator+( point a, point b)
{
        point temp;
        temp.x = a.x + b.y;
        temp.y = a.y + b.y;
        return temp;
}
istream& operator>> (istream& in, point &p)
{
        cout<<"\n enter x:";
        in >> p.x ;
        cout<<"\n enter y:";
        in>>p.y;
        return in;
}
ostream& operator<< ( ostream &out, point &p)
{
        out<<" \n ( "<<p.x<< " ' "<<p.y<<" ) ";
}
int main()
{
        point p1,p2;
        cout<<" \n enter data for p1:";
        cin>>p1;
        cout<<"\n enter data for p2:";
        cin>>p2;
        point p3;
        p3=p1+p2;
        cout<<p1;
        cout<<p2;
        cout<<p3;
        return 0;
}
```

Rules for Overloading Operator:-

⇒ Although it looks simple to redefine the operators, there are certain restrictions and limitations in overloading them. Some of them are listed below:

1. Only existing operators can be overloaded. New operators cannot be created.
2. The overloaded operator must have at least one operand that is of user-defined type.
3. We cannot change the basic meaning of an operator. That is to say, we cannot redefine the plus(+) operator to subtract one value from the other.
4. Overloaded operators follow the syntax rules of the original operators. They cannot be overridden.
5. There are some operators that cannot be overloaded.

Sizeof	Size of operator
.	Membership operator
.*	Pointer-to-member operator
::	Scope resolution operator
?:	Conditional operator

Operators that cannot be overloaded

6. We cannot use friend functions to overload following operators. However member function can be used to overload them.

=	Assignment operator
()	Function call operator
[]	Subscripting operator
->	Class member access operator

7. Unary operators, overloaded by means of a member function, take no explicit arguments and return no explicit values, but, those overloaded by means of a friend function, take one reference argument.
8. Binary operators, overloaded by means of a member function, take one explicit argument, but, those overloaded by means of a friend function, take two reference arguments.
9. When using binary operators overloaded through a member function, the left hand operand must be an object of the relevant class.
10. Binary arithmetic operators such as +, -, *, / must explicitly return a value. They must not attempt to change their own arguments.

6.2 Type Conversion:-

⇒ Since the user-defined data types are designed by us to suit our requirements, the compiler does not support automatic type conversions for such data types.

⇒ We must, therefore, design the conversion routines by ourselves, if such operations are required.

⇒ Three types of situations might arise in the data conversion between incompatible types:

1. ***Conversion from basic type to class type.***
2. ***Conversion from class type to basic type.***
3. ***Conversion from one class type to another class type.***

1. Basic to Class Type:-

⇒ The conversion from basic type to class type is easy to accomplish.

⇒ For example, a constructor was used to build a string type object from char* type variable.

⇒ The following example illustrate the conversion from char* to string type.

```
#include<iostream.h>
#include<string.h>
class string
{
  private:
        char * str;
        int l;
  public:
        string()
        {
              l=0;
              str = new char[l+1];
        }
        string( char *n)
        {
              l= strlen(n);
              str= new char[l+1];
              strcpy(str,n);
        }
        void display()
        {
              cout<<"\n string="<<str;
        }
};
```

```
int main()
{
        string s1;
        char* n="hello";
        s1=n;               //conversion from char* to string
        s1.display();
        return 0;
}
```

2. Class to Basic type:-

⇒ C++ allows us to define an overloaded casting operator that could be used to convert a class type data to a basic type. The general form of an overloaded casting operator function, usually referred to as a conversion function, is:

```
operator typename()
{
        .........
        ......... ( function statements)
        .........
}
```

⇒ This function converts a class type data to typename. For example, the operator double() converts a class object to type double, the operator int() converts a class type object to type int.

⇒ The casting operator function should satisfy the following conditions:

- It must be a class member.
- It must not specify a return type.
- It must not have any arguments.

⇒ Since it is a member function, it is invoked by the object and, therefore, the values used for conversion inside the function belong to the object that invoked the function. This means that the function does not need an argument.

⇒ The example is given with the next topic.

3. One Class to Another Class Type:-

⇒ We have just seen data conversion techniques from a basic to class type and a class to basic type. But there are situations where we would like to convert one class type data to another class type.

⇒ For example,

objX = objY; //objects of different types.

objX is an object of class X and objY is an object of class Y. the class Y type data is converted to the class X type data and the converted value is assigned to the objX.

⇒ Since the conversion takes place from class Y to class X, Y is known as the **source class** and X is known as the **destination class**.

⇒ Such conversion between objects of different classes can be carried out by <u>either a constructor or a conversion function</u>.

⇒ We know that the casting operator function operator typename() converts the class object of which it is a member to typename. The typename amy be a built-in type or a user-defined one.

⇒ In the case of conversions between objects, typename refers to the destination class. Therfore, when a class needs to be converted, a casting operator function can be used. The conversion takes place in the source class and the result is given to the destination class object.

⇒ Now consider a single argument constructor function which servec as an instruction for converting the argument's type to the class and is passed to the destination class for conversion.

⇒ The figure illustrates these two approaches.

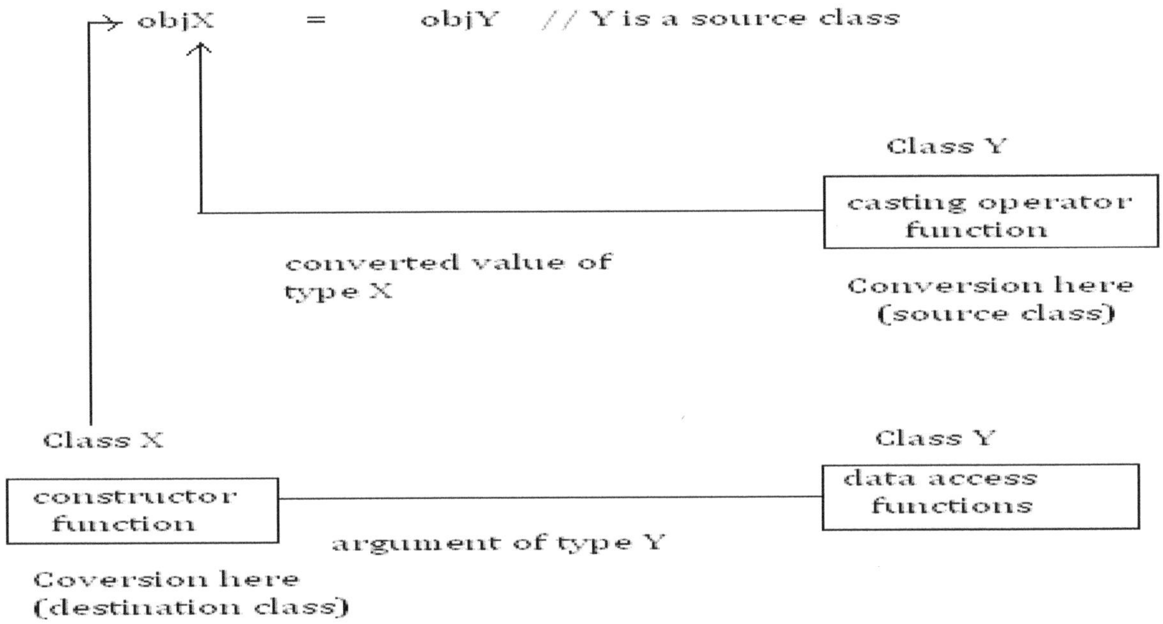


```
// program to conver one class type to another using constructor.
#include<iostream.h>
class invent2;              //destination class declared
class invent1
{
    private:
        int code;
        int items;
        float price;
    public:
        invent1(int a, int b, float c)
        {
            code=a;
            items=b;
```

```
                price=c;
            }
            void putdata()
            {
                cout<<"\n code="<<code<<"\n
items="<<items<<"\nprice="<<price;
            }
            int getcode()
            {
                return code;
            }
            int getitems()
            {
                return items;
            }
            int getprice()
            {
                return price;
            }
            operator float()
            {
                reurn items*price;
            }
        };
        class invent2
        {
            private:
                int code;
                float value;
            public:
                invent2()
                {
                    code=value=0;
                }
                invent2(int x, float y)
                {
                    code=x;
                    value=y;
                }
                intvent2(invent1 p)
                {
                    code= p.getcode();
                    value= getitems() * getprice();
                }
                void putdata()
                {
```

```
                    cout<<"\n code="<<code<<"\n value="<<value;
                }
};
int main()
{
        invent1 i1(100,5,10);
        intvent2 i2;
        float total_amt;


        total_amt=i1;               //conversion from invent1 to float
        i2=i1;              //conversion from invent2 to invent1


        i1.putdata();
        cout<<"\n total amount="<<total_amt;
        i2.putdata();

        return 0;
}

// program to conver one class type to another using operator function..
#include<iostream.h>
class invent2;              //destination class declared
class invent1
{
        private:
                int code;
                int items;
                float price;
        public:
                invent1(int a, int b, float c)
                {
                        code=a;
                        items=b;
                        price=c;
                }
                void putdata()
                {
                        cout<<"\n code="<<code<<"\n
items="<<items<<"\nprice="<<price;
                }
                operator invent2()
                {
                        invent2 temp(code,(items*price));
                        return temp;
```

```
		}
		operator float()
		{
			reurn items*price;
		}
	};
	class invent2
	{
		private:
			int code;
			float value;
		public:
			invent2()
			{
				code=value=0;
			}

			invent2(int x, float y)
			{
				code=x;
				value=y;
			}
			intvent2(invent1 p)
			{
				code= p.getcode();
				value= getitems() * getprice();
			}
			void putdata()
			{
				cout<<"\n code="<<code<<"\n value="<<value;
			}
};
int main()
{
	invent1 i1(100,5,10);
	intvent2 i2;
	float total_amt;

	 total_amt=i1;			//conversion from invent1 to float

	i2=i1;			//conversion from invent2 to invent1
	i1.putdata();
	cout<<"\n total amount="<<total_amt;
	i2.putdata();
	return 0;
}
```

Unit - 7

Inheritance

7.1 Introduction :

- Reusability is yet another important feature of OOP.
- It is always nice if we could reuse something that already exists rather than trying to create the same all over again. It would not only save time and money but also reduce frustration and increase reliability.
- For instance, the reuse of a class that has already been tested, debugged and used many times can save us the effort of developing and testing the same again.
- Fortunately, C++ strongly supports the concept of ***reusability.***
- The C++ classes can be reused in several ways. Once a class has been written and tested, it can be adapted by other programmers to suit their requirements. This is basically done by creating new classes, reusing the properties of the existing ones.
- ***The mechanism of deriving a new class from an old one is called inheritance (or derivation). The old class is referred to as the base class and the new one is called the derived class or subclass.***
- The derived class inherits some or all of the traits from the base class.
- A class can also inherit properties from more than one class or from more than one level.
- A derived class with only one base class is called ***single inheritance*** and one with several base classes is called ***multiple inheritance***.
- On the other hand, the traits of one class may be inherited by more than one class. This process is known as ***hierarchical inheritance.***
- The mechanism of deriving a class from another 'derived class' is known as ***multilevel inheritance***.
- Following figure shows various forms of inheritance that could be used for writing extensible programs. The direction of arrow indicates the direction of inheritance. (Some authors show the opposite direction meaning inherited from.)

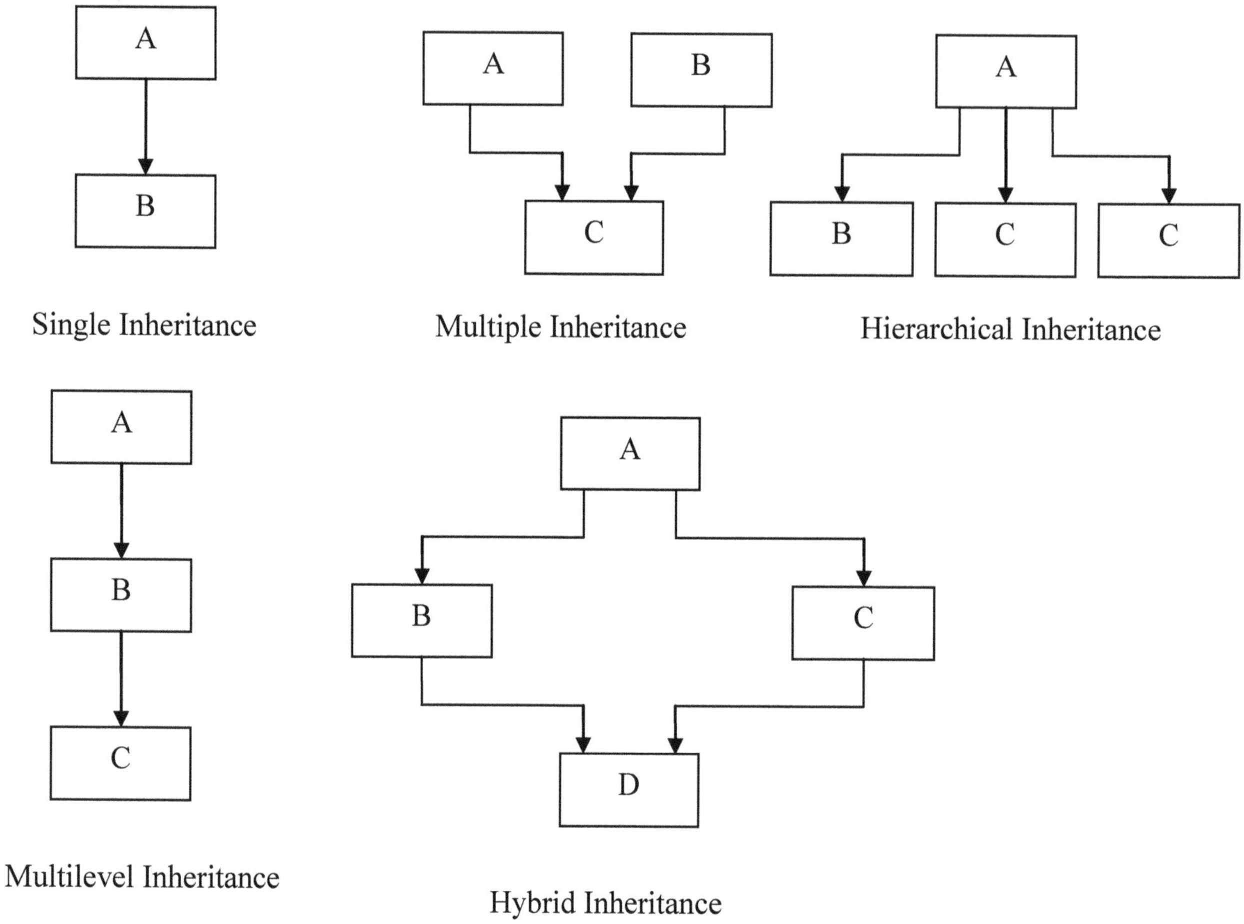

Forms Of Inheritance

7.2 Defining Derived Classes:

A derived class can be defined by specifying its relationship with the base class in addition to its own details. The general form of defining a derived class is:

```
class derived-class-name : visibility-mode base-class-name
{
        .....
        ..... // members of derived class
        .....
};
```

The colon indicates that the ***derived-class-name*** is derived from the ***base-class-name.*** The ***visibility-mode*** is optional and, if present, may be either **private or public.** The default visibility-mode is **private.** Visibility mode specifies whether the features of the base class ***privately derived or publicly derived.***

Examples:

```
class ABC : private XYZ
{
        members of ABC
};
class ABC :  public XYZ
{
        members of ABC
};
```

- When a base class ***is privately inherited*** by a derived class, **'public members'** of the base **class** become **'private members'** of the derived class and therefore the public members of the base class can only be accessed by the member functions of the derived class.
- They are inaccessible to the objects of the derived class. Remember, a public member of a class can be accessed by its own objects using the ***dot operator.*** The result is that no member of the base class is accessible to the objects of the derived class.
- On the other hand, when the base class ***is publicly inherited,*** **'public members'** of the class become **'public members'** of the derived class and therefore they are accessible to the objects of the derived class. In ***both the cases, the private members are not inherited*** and therefore, the private members of a base class will never become the members of its derived class.
- In inheritance, some of the base class data elements and member functions are 'inherited' into the derived class. We can add our own data and member functions and thus extend the functionality of the base class. Inheritance, when used to modify and extend the functionality of the existing classes, becomes a very powerful tool for incremental program development.

7.3 Single Inheritance:

- Let us consider a simple example to illustrate inheritance. Following program shows a base class B and a derived class D, The class B contains one private data member, one public data member, and three public member functions. The class D contains one private data member and two public member functions.

```
#include <iostream.h>
class B
{
```

```
    int a;
    public:
    int b;
    void get_ab();
    int get_a(void);
    void show a(void);
};
void B :: get_ab(void)
{
        a = 5;
        b = 10;
}
int B :: get_a( )
{
        return a;
}
void B :: snow_a( )
{
        cout  «  "a = " « a « "\n";
}

class  D   :   public  B
{
     int c;
     public:
     void mul (void);
     void display (void);
};
void D :: mul()
{
    c = b * get_a( );
}
void  D :: display( )
{
      cout     « "a =       "  « get_a() « "\n";
      cout     « "b =       "  « b  « "\n";
      cout     « "c =       " « c « "\n\n";
}

int main ()
{
        D d;
        d.get_ab ( );
        d.mul ();
        d.show_a ();
        d.display ( );
```

```
        d.b = 20;
        d.mul ();
        d.display ();
        return 0;
}
```

Given below is the output of above program

```
a = 5
a = 5
b = 10
c = 50

a = 5
b = 20
c = 100
```

- The class D is a public derivation of the base class B. Therefore, D inherits all the public members of B and retains their visibility. Thus a public member of the base class B is also a public member of the derived class D. The private members of B cannot be inherited by D. The class D, in effect, will have more members than what it contains at the time of declaration as shown in following Fig.

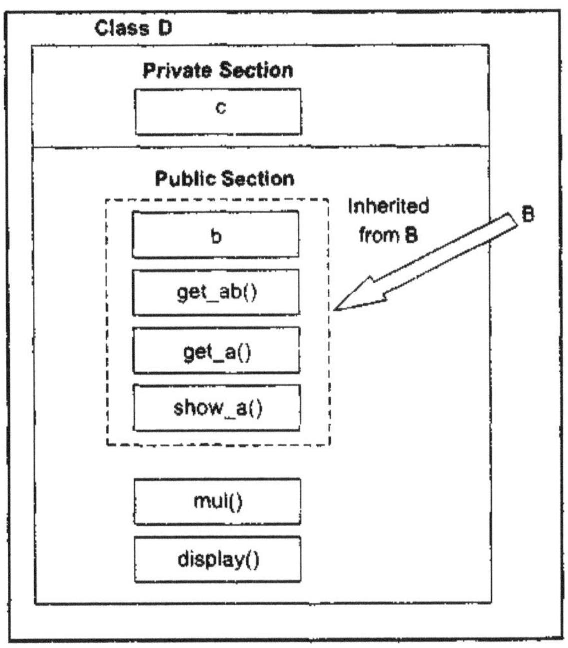

Adding more members to a class (by public derivation)

- The program illustrates that the objects of class D have access to all the public members of B. Let us have a look at the functions **show_a( ) and mul( ):**

```
void show_a()
{
        cout « "a =  " « a « "\n";
}
 void mul ( )
{
        c = b * get_a();    // c = b * a;
}
```

- Although the data member a is private in B and cannot be inherited, objects of D are able to access it through an inherited member function of B.

- Let us now consider the case of private derivation.

```
#include <iostream.h>
class B
{
    int a;
    public:
    int b;
    void get_ab();
    int get_a(void);
    void show a(void);
};
void B :: get_ab(void)
{
        a = 5;
        b = 10;
}
int B :: get_a( )
{
        return a;
}
void B :: snow_a( )
{
        cout  «  "a = " « a « "\n";
}
class  D  :  private B              //private derivation
{
     int c;
     public:
     void mul (void);
     void display (void);
};
```

```
void D :: mul()
{
   c = b * get_a( );
}
void  D :: display( )
{
  cout    « "a =      "  « get_a() « "\n";
  cout    « "b =      "  « b  « "\n";
  cout    « "c =      " « c « "\n\n";
}
int main ()
{
        D d;
        d.get_ab ( );
        d.mul ();
        d.show_a ();
        d.display ( );
        // d.b = 20;          Not work; b has become private
        d.mul ();
        d.display ();
        return 0;
}
```

- The membership of the derived class D is shown in following Fig. In **private** derivation, the public members of the base class become **private** members of the derived class. Therefore, D cannot have direct access to the public member functions of B.

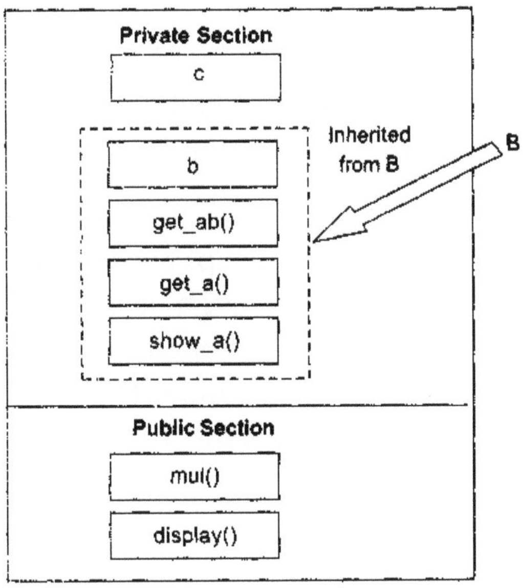

Adding more members to a class (by private derivation)

Making a Private Member Inheritable:

- We have just seen how to increase the capabilities of an existing class without modifying it. We have also seen that a private member of a base class cannot be inherited; it is not available for the derived class directly.
- What do we do if the **private** data member be inherited by a derived class? This can be accomplished by modifying the visibility limit of the **private** member by making it **public.** This would make it accessible to all the functions of the program, thus taking away the advantage of data hiding.
- C++ provides a third visibility modifier, **protected,** which serve a limited purpose in inheritance.
    - A member declared as **protected** is accessible by the member functions within its class and any class immediately derived from it. It cannot be accessed by the functions outside these two classes. A class can now use all the three visibility modes as illustrated below.

```
class alpha
{
        private:      //      optional
                ... ... //      within its class
                ... ...
        protected :
                ... ... //      visible to members functions
                ... ... //      of its own and derived class
        public :
                ... ... //      visible to all functions
                ... ... //      in the program
};
```

- When a **protected** member is inherited in public mode, it becomes **protected** in the derived class too and therefore is accessible by the member functions of the derived class. It is also ready for further inheritance.
- A protected member indented in the **private** mode derivation, becomes **private** in the derived class. Although it is available to the member functions of the derived class, it is not available for further inheritance (since **private members** cannot be inherited). Following Figure is the pictorial representation for the two levels of derivation.

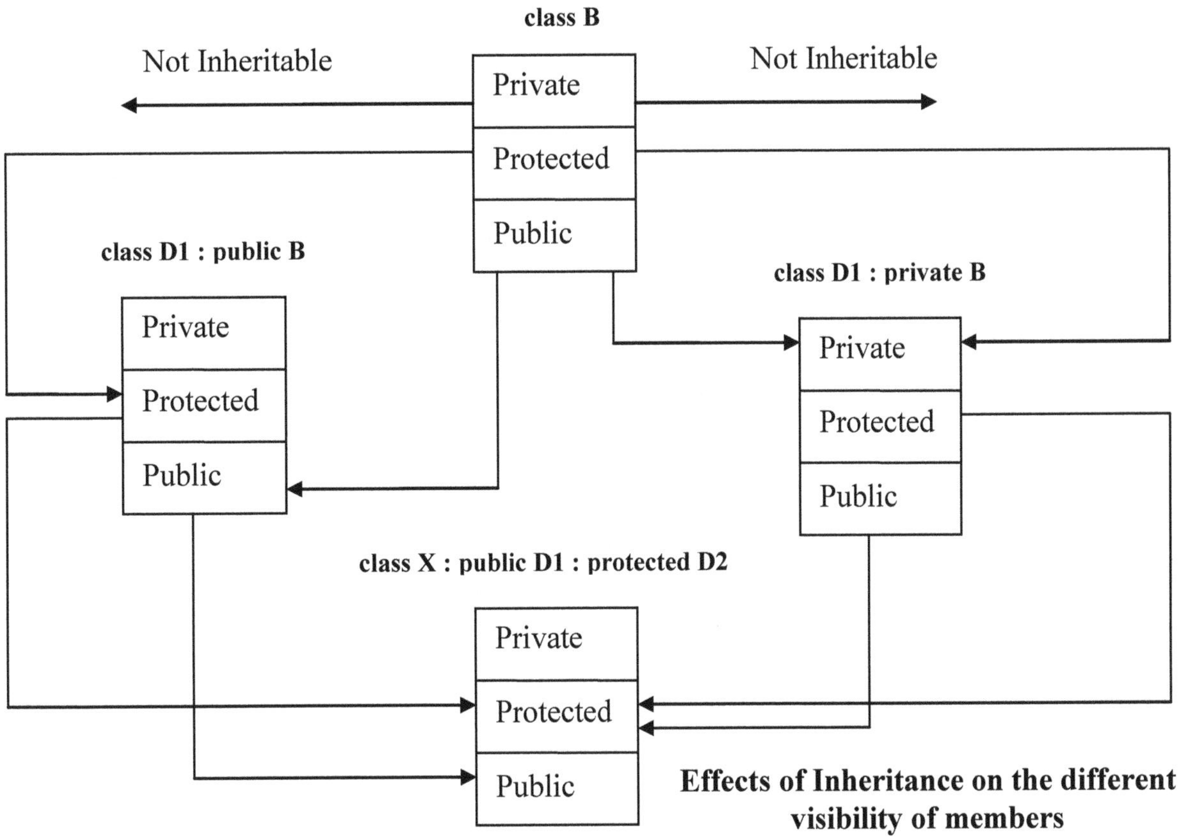

Effects of Inheritance on the different visibility of members

- The keywords private, protected, and public may appear in any order and any numbers of times in the declaration of class. It is also possible a base class in protected mode known as protected derivation.
- In protected derivation, both the public and protected members of the base class become protected members of the derived class. Following table summarizes how the visibility of base class members undergoes modification in all three types of derivation.
- Now let review the access control to the private and protected members of a class. What are the various functions that can have access to these members?

    1. ***A function that is a friend of the class.***
    2. ***A member function of a class that is a friend of the class.***
    3. ***A member function of a derived class.***

- While the friend function and the member functions of a friend class can have direct access to both the private and protected data, the member functions of a derived class can directly access only the protected data. However they can access the private data through the member functions of the base class.

Base class visibility	Derived class visibility		
	public derivation	private derivation	protected derivation
Private	Not inherited	Not inherited	Not inherited
Protected	protected	private	protected
public	public	private	protected

--- Visibility of inherited members ---

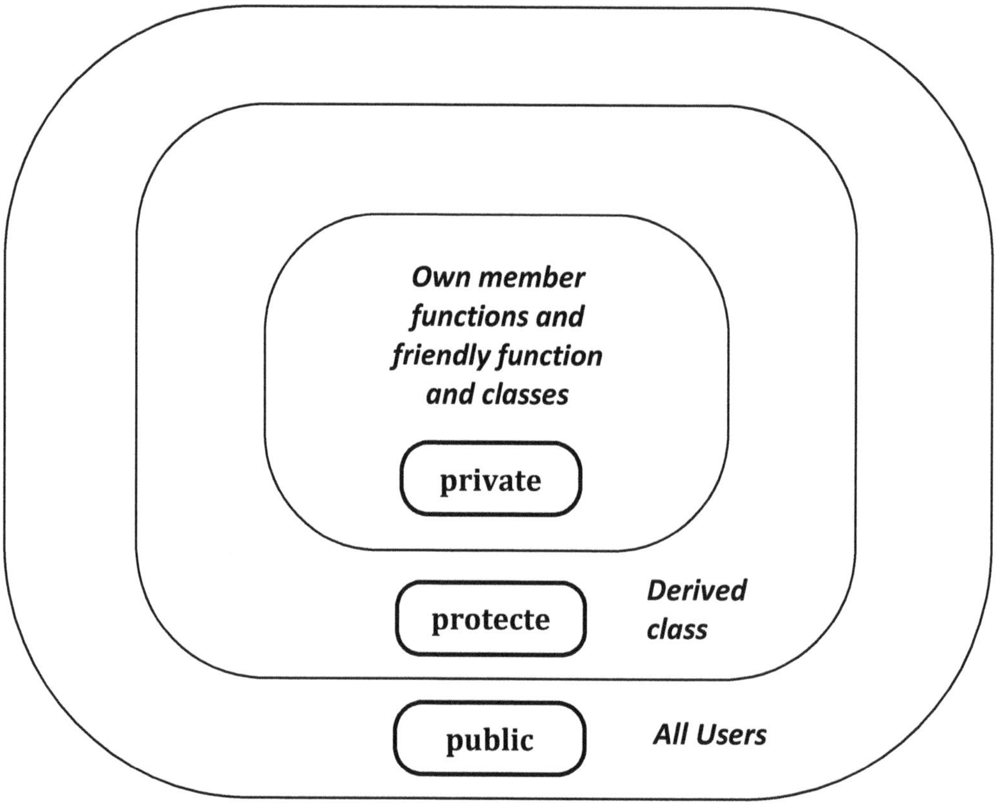

A simple view of access control to the members of a class.

7.4 Multilevel Inheritance:

- A class is inherited from a base class which in turn inherited from another base class

```
#include<iostreaam.h>
class student
{
        protected:
```

```
            int roll_number;
        public:
            void get_number(int a)
            {
                roll_number = a;
            }
            void put_number ( )
            {
                cout << "Roll Number : " << roll_number << "\n';
            }
};

class test :: public student
{
        protected:
            float sub1;
            float sub2;
        public:
        void get_marks (float x, float y)
        {
            sub1 = x;
            sub2 = y;
        }
        void put_marks( )
        {
            cout << "Marks in subject 1 : " << sub1 << "\n";
            cout << "Marks in subject 2 : " << sub2 << "\n";
        }
};

class result : public test
{
        float total;
        public :
            void display(void)
            {
                total = sub1 + sub2;
                put_number ( );
                put_marks ( );
                cout << "Total = " <<  total < "\n";
            }
};
int main( )
{
        result student1;
        student1.get_number(111);
```

```
        student1.get_marks(75.0, 59.5);
        student1.display( );
}
```

7.5 Multiple inheritances:

- A class can inherit the attribute of two or more classes is known as multiple inheritance.
  For example :

```
#include<iostream.h>
class M
{
        protected:
                int m;
        public :
        void get_m(int x)
        {
                m = x;
        }
};

class N
{
        protected:
                int n;
        public :
        void get_n(int y)
        {
                n = y;
        }
};

class P : public M, public N
{
        public :
        void display ( )
        {
                cou << "m = " << m << "\n";
                cou << "n = " << n << "\n";
                cou << "m * n = " << m * n << "\n";
        }
};

int main( )
{
```

```
        P p;

        p.get_m(10);
        p.get_n(20);
        p.display( );

        return 0;
}
```

Ambiguity resolution in inheritance:

- In using multiple inheritance where a function with the same name appears in more than one base class then it can be resolved using scope resolution operator.

  i.e. M :: display() ; N :: display( );

Hierarchical Inheritance:

- We have discussed so far how inheritance can be used to modify a class when it did not satisfy the requirements of a particular problem on hand.
- Additional members are added through inheritance to extend the capabilities of a class.
- Another interesting application of inheritance is a support to the hierarchical design of a program. Many programming problems can be cast, into a hierarchy where certain features of one level shared by many others below that level
- As an example following Fig. shows a hierarchical classification of students in a university. Another example could be the classification of accounts in a commercial bank as shown in second Fig.

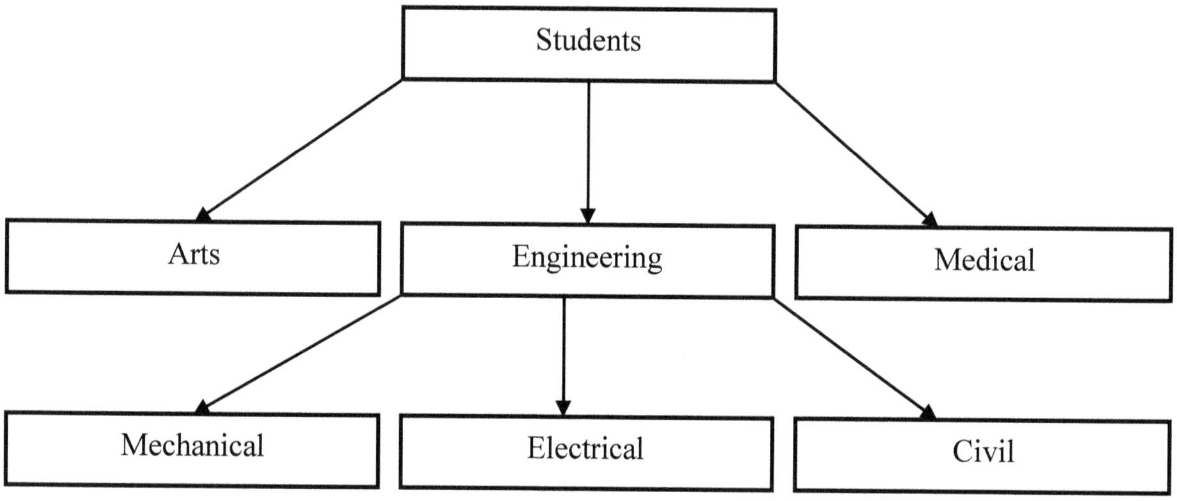

Hierarchical classification of students

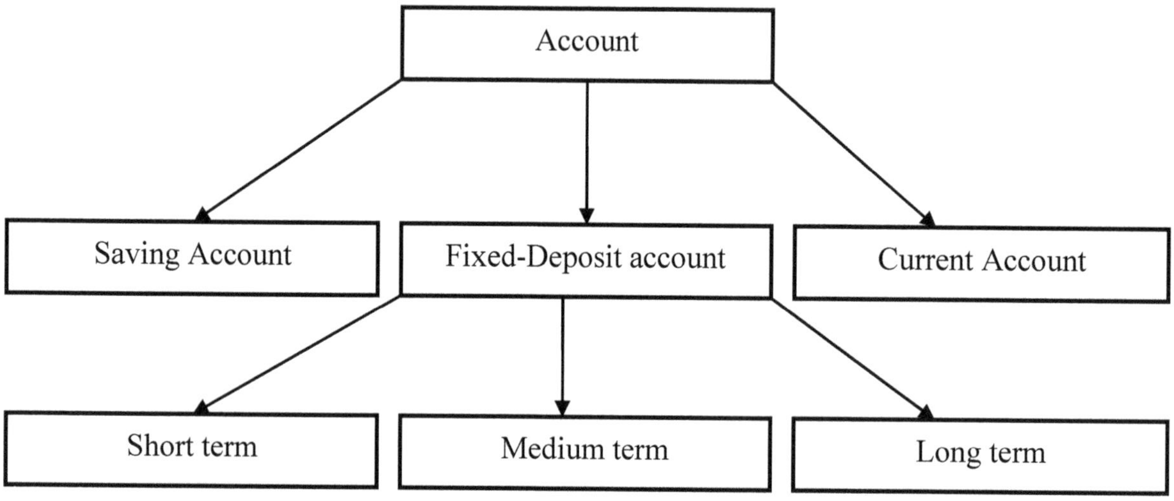

Hierarchical classification of bank accounts

- In **C++** such a classification problems can be easily converted into a class hierarchies. The base class will include the features that are common to the subclasses. A subclass can be constructed by inheriting the properties of the base class. A subclass can serve as a base class for the lower classes and so on.

Hybrid inheritance:

- There could be situations where we need to apply two or more type of inheritance to design a program.
- For example consider the student result discussed above. Assume that we have to give weightage for sports before finalizing the results. The

weightage for sports stored in a separate class called sports. The new inheritance relationship between the various classes would be as shown in following figure.

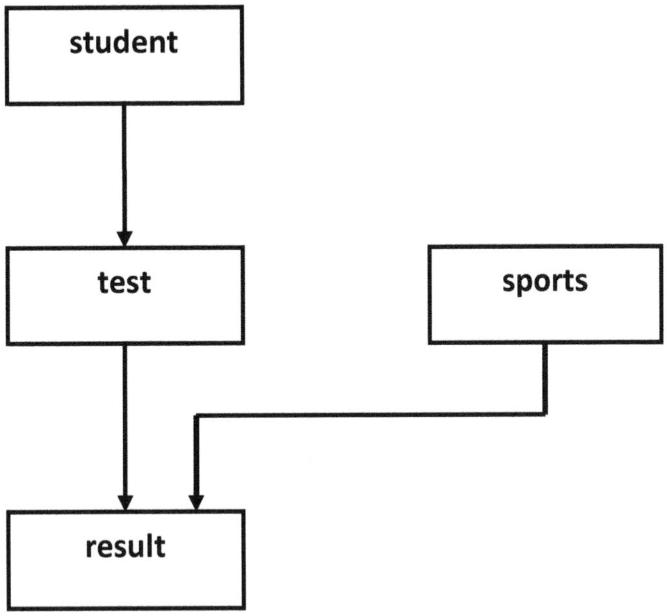

Hybrid Inheritance : Multilevel , Multiple and Hierarchical Inheritance

Example Program:

```
#include<iostreaam.h>
class student
{
        protected:
                int roll_number;
        public:
                void get_number(int a)
                {
                        roll_number = a;
                }
                void put_number ( )
                {
                        cout << "Roll Number : " << roll_number << "\n';
                }
};

class test :: public student
{
        protected:
                float sub1;
                float sub2;
        public:
```

```
        void get_marks (float x, float y)
        {
                sub1 = x;
                sub2 = y;
        }
        void put_marks( )
        {
                cout << "Marks in subject 1 : " << sub1 << "\n";
                cout << "Marks in subject 2 : " << sub2 << "\n";
        }
};

class sports
{
        protected:
                float score;
        public:
                void get_score (float s)
                {
                        score = s;
                }
                void put_score ( )
                {
                        cout << "Sports weight : " << score << "\n';
                }
};

class result : public test, public sports
{
        float total;
        public :
                void display(void)
                {
                        total = sub1 + sub2 + score;
                        put_number ( );
                        put_marks ( );
                        put_total ( );
                        cout << "Total  Score= " <<  total < "\n";
                }
};


int main( )
{
        result student1;
        student1.get_number (1234);
```

```
        student1.get_marks (27.50, 33.0);
        student1.get_score(6.);
        student1.display ( );
    }
```

Virtual Base Classes:

- We have just discussed a situation which would require the use of both the multiple and multilevel inheritance.
- Consider a situation where all the three kinds of inherits multilevel, multiple and hierarchical inheritance, are involved.
- This is illustrated in following Fig. The **'child'** has two ***direct base classes*** **'parent1' and 'parent2'** which' have a common base class **'grandparent'.** The **'child'** inherits the traits of **'grandparent'** two separate paths. It can also inherit directly as shown by the broken line. The **'grandparent'** is sometimes referred to as ***indirect base class.***

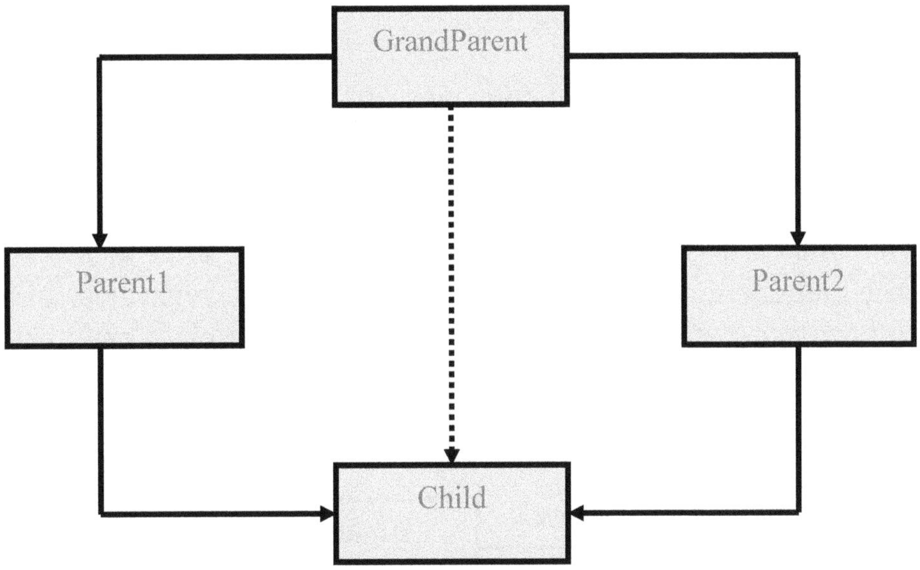

Multipath Inheritance

- Inheritance by the **'child'** as shown in above Fig. might pose some problems. All the public and protected members of **'grandparent'** are inherited into **'child'** twice, first via **'parent1'** and again via **'parent2'**. This means, **'child'** would have ***duplicate*** sets of the members inherited from **'grandparent'**. This introduces ambiguity and should be avoided.
- The duplication of inherited members due to these multiple paths can be avoided by using the common base class (ancestor class) as ***virtual base class*** while declaring the direct or intermediate base classes as shown below:

```
Class A     //     grandparent
```

```
{
        ... ...
        ... ...
};

class B1 : virtual public A       //      parent1
{
        ... ...
        ... ...
};

class B2 : public virtual A       //      parent2
{
        ... ...
        ... ...
};

class C : public B1, public B2
{
        ... ...        //      only one copy of A will be inherited
        ... ...
};
```

- When a class is made a virtual base class, C++ takes necessary care to see that only one copy of that class is inherited, regardless of how many inheritance paths exist between the virtual base class and a friend classes.
- A program to implement the concept of virtual base class is given below.

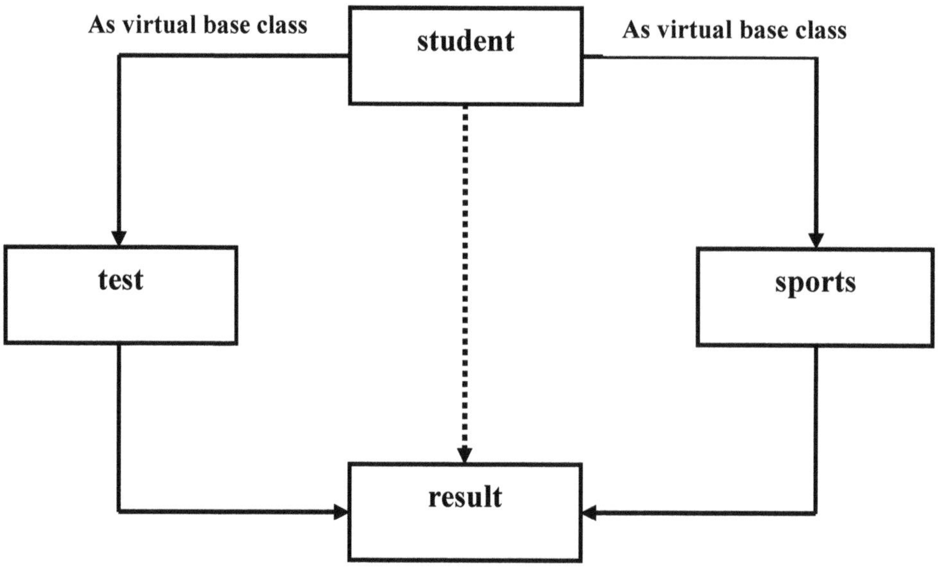

Multipath Inheritance : Virtual base class

```
#include<iostre
class student
```

```
{
   protected:
          int roll_number;
   public:
          void get_number(int a)
          {
                 roll_number = a;
          }
          void put_number ( )
          {
                 cout << "Roll Number : " << roll_number << "\n';
          }
};

class test :: virtual public student
{
   protected:
          float sub1;
          float sub2;
   public:
   void get_marks (float x, float y)
   {
          sub1 = x;
          sub2 = y;
   }
   void put_marks ( )
   {
          cout << "Marks in subject 1 : " << sub1 << "\n";
          cout << "Marks in subject 2 : " << sub2 << "\n";
   }
};

class sports : public virtual student
{
   protected:
          float score;
   public:
          void get_score (float s)
          {
                 score = s;
          }
          void put_score ( )
          {
                 cout << "Sports weight : " << score << "\n';
          }
};
```

```
class result : public test, public sports
{
   float total;
   public :
           void display(void)
           {
                   total = sub1 + sub2 + score;
                   put_number ( );
                   put_marks ( );
                       put_total ( );
                   cout << "Total  Score= " << total < "\n";
           }
};
int main( )
{
   result student1;
   student1.get_number (678);
   student1.get_marks (30.50, 25.5);
       student1.get_score (7.0);
   student1.display ( );
}
```

Abstract Classes

- An ***abstract*** class is one that is not used to create objects. An abstract class is designed to act as a base class (to be inherited by other classes). It is a design concept in program development and provides a base upon which other classes may be built. In student's result example, the student class is an abstract class since it was not used to create any object.

Constructors in Derived Classes

- As we know, the constructors play an important role in initializing objects. We did not use them earlier in the derived classes for the sake of simplicity.
- One important thing to note here is that as long as no base class constructor takes any arguments, the derived class need not have a constructor function.
- However, if any base class contains a constructor with one or more arguments, then it is ***mandatory*** for the derived class to have a constructor **and** pass the arguments to the base class constructors. Remember, while applying inheritance we usually create objects using the derived class. Thus, it makes sense for the derived class to pass arguments to the base class constructor. When both the derived and base classes contain constructors, the base constructor is

executed first and then the constructor in the derived class is executed.

- In case of multiple inheritances, the base classes are constructed ***in the order in which they appear in the declaration of the derived class.*** Similarly, in a multilevel inheritance, the constructors will be executed ***in the order of inheritance.***
- Since the derived class takes the responsibility of supplying initial values to its base classes, we supply the initial values that are required by all the classes together, when a derived class object is declared. How are they passed to the base class constructors so that they can do their job? C++ supports a special argument passing mechanism for such situations.
- The constructor of the derived class receives the entire list of values as its arguments and passes them on to the base constructors in the order in which they are declared in the derived class. The base constructors are called and executed before executing the statement of the derived constructor.
- General form of defining a derived constructor is:

```
Derived – constructor (arglist1, arglist2, … … arglistN, arglist(D)) :
        base1(arglist1),
        base2(arglist2),
        … …
        … …
        baseN(arglistN),
{
        Body of derived constructor
}
```

- The header line ***of derived-constructor*** function contains two parts separated by a colon (:). The first part provides the declaration of the arguments that are passed to the base class constructors and the second part lists the function calls to the base constructors.
- *Base1(arglist1), base2(arglist2) … …* are function calls to base constructors base1( ), base2( ), … … and therefore arglist1, arglist2,… …. arglistN etc. represent the actual parameters that are passed to the base class constructors. Arglistl through arglistN are the argument declarations for base class constructors basel through baseN. arglistD provides the parameters that are necessary to initialize the members of the derived class.

Example:

```
D (int al, int a2, float b1, float b2, int dl):
A (a1, a2),    /* call to constructor A */
B (bl, b2)     /* call to constructor B *,/
```

```
{
  d = dl;  // executes its own body
}
```

- A(al, a2) invokes the base constructor A( ) and B(bl,b2) invokes another base class constructor B( ). The constructor D ( ) supplies the values for these four arguments. In addition it has one argument of its own. The constructor D ( ) has a total of five arguments. D ( ) may be invoked as follows:

  … …
  D objD (5, 12, 2.5, 7.54, 30);

Method of Inheritance	**Order of execution**

Class B : public A
{
};
	A( ); Base constructor
	B( ); Derived constructor

Class A : public B, public C
{
};
	B( ); Base constructor first
	C( ); Base constructor first
	A ( ); Derived constructor

Class A : public B, virtual public C
{
};
	C( ); Virtual Base constructor first
	C( ); Ordinary Base constructor first
	A ( ); Derived constructor

Execution of base class constructors.

```
#include<iostream.h>
class alpha
{
        int x;
        public :
        alpha(int i)
        {
                x = i;
                cout << "alpha initialized \n";
        }
        void show_x (void)
        {
                cout << "x = " << x << "\n";
        }
};

class beta
{
        int p, q;
        public :
        beta (int j)
```

```
        {
                y = j;
                cout << "beta initialized \n";
        }
        void show_y (void)
        {
                cout << "y = " << y << "\n";
        }
};
class gamma : public beta, public alpha
{
        int m, n;
        public :
        gamma (int a, int b, int c, int d) :
        alpha(a), beta(b)
        {
                m = c;
                n = d;
                cout << "gamma initialized \n";
        }
        void show_mn (void)
        {
                cout << "x = " << x << "\n";
        }
};
int main( )
{
        gamma g(5, 10.75, 20, 30);

        cout << "\n";
        g.show_x ( );
        g.show_y ( );
        g.show_mn ( );
        return 0;
}
```

- Here in above example beta is initialized first, although it appears second in the derived class because it has been declared first in the derived class header line. Output will be as follows

    beta initialized

    alpha initialized

    gamma initialized

    x = 5

    y = 10.75

m = 20

n = 30

C++ supports another method of initialization as given code below.

```
#include<iostream.h>
class alpha
{
        int x;
        public :
        alpha (int i)
        {
                x = i;
                cout << "alpha initialized \n";
        }
        void show_alpha (void)
        {
                cout << "x = " << x << "\n";
        }
};

class beta
{
        float p, q;
        public :
        beta (float a, float b) : p(a), q(b+p)
        {
                cout << "beta initialized \n";
        }
        void show_beta (void)
        {
                cout << "p = " << p << "\n";
                cout << "q = " << q << "\n";
        }
};

class gamma : public beta, public alpha
{
        int u, v;
        public :
        gamma (int a, int b, float c) :
        alpha(a *  2), beta(c, c), u(a)
        {
                v = b;
                cout << "gamma initialized \n";
        }
        void show_gamma (void)
```

```
        {
                cout << "u = " << u << "\n";
                cout << "v = " << v << "\n";
        }
};
int main( )
{
        gamma g(2, 4, 2.50);

        cout << "Display member values.\n";

        g.show_alpha ( );
        g.show_beta ( );
        g.show_gamma ( );

        return 0;
}
```

Here is the output:

```
beta initialized
alpha initialized
gamma initialized
x = 4
y = 2.5
p = 5
q = 2
u = 2
v = 4
```

- The argument list of the gamma constructor **gamma** contains only three parameters a, b, and c which are used to initialize the five members contained in all the three classes.

Member Classes: Nesting of Classes

- Inheritance is the mechanism of deriving certain properties of one class into another.
- We have seen in detail how this is implemented using the concept of derived classes.
- C++ supports vet another way of inheriting properties of one class into another. This approach takes a view that an object can be a collection of many other objects.
- That is, a class a class can contain objects of other classes as its members as shown below:

```
class alpha {....};
class beta {....};
```

```
class gamma
{
        alpha a;
        beta b;
};
```

- All objects of **gamma** class will contain the objects a and b. This kind of relationship is called ***containership*** or ***nesting.***
- Creation of an object that contains another object is very different than the creation of an independent object. An independent object is created by its constructor when it is declared with arguments. On the other hand, a nested object is created in two stages. First, the member objects are created using their respective constructors and then the other 'ordinary' members are created.
- This means, constructors of all the objects should be called before its own constructor body is executed. This is accomplished by using an initialization list in the constructor of the nested class.

  Example:

```
class gamma
{
        ... ...
        alpha a;   // a is object of alpha
        beta b;            // b is object of beta
        public :
        gamma (arglist) : a(arglist1, arglist(2)
        {
           // constructor body
        }
};
```

- arglist is the list of arguments that is to be supplied when a gamma object is defined. These parameters are used for initializing the members of gamma. arglist1 is the argument list for the constructor of a and arglist2 is the argument list for the constructor of b. arglist1 and arglist2 may or may not use the arguments from arglist. Remember, a(arglist1) and b(arglist2) are function calls and therefore the arguments do not contain the data types. They are simply be variables or constants.

  Example:

```
gamma (int x, int y, int z) : a(x), b(x, z)
{
  // constructor body
  // Assignment section for ordinary the members
}
```

- We can use as many member objects as are required in a class. For each member object we add constructor call in the initializer list. The constructors of the member objects are called in the order in which they are declared in the nested class.

Unit - 8
Pointers, Virtual Functions and Polymorphism

8.1 Introduction :

- ✓ Polymorphism simply means 'same name many forms'.
- ✓ We have already seen the concept of polymorphism in operator overloading and function overloading.
- ✓ The overloaded member functions are selected for invoking by matching arguments, both type and number.
- ✓ This information is known to the compiler at the compile time and therefore compiler is able to select the appropriate function for a particular all the compile time itself. This is called early binding or static binding or static linking or compile time polymorphism.
- ✓ Early binding simply means that an object is bound to its function call at compile time.
- ✓ Now consider the case where we have the same function name and prototype in both the base and derived classes.
- ✓ We have seen earlier that, in such a situation, we may use the class resolution operator to specify the class while invoking the function with the derived class object.
- ✓ It would be nice if the appropriate member function could be selected while the program is running.
- ✓ This is known as run time polymorphism and it is achieved by virtual function in C++.

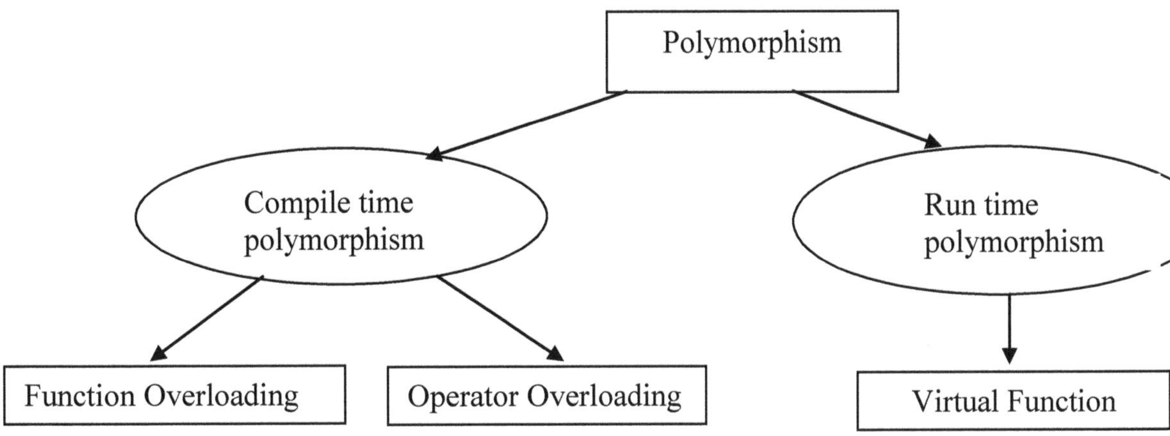

- ✓ At run time, when it is known what class objects are under consideration, the appropriate version of the function in invoked.
- ✓ Since the function is linked with a particular class much after the compilation, this process is known as late binding or dynamic binding because the selection of the appropriate function is done dynamically at run time.
- ✓ Dynamic binding requires the use of pointer to objects.

8.2 Pointer to Objects :

- ✓ Pointer can be used to hold addresses of objects, just as they can hold addresses of primitive and user defined data items.

- ✓ Consider the statement,

```
Item x;
```

- ✓ Where Item is a class and x is an object defined to be of type Item. Similarly we can define a pointer ptr of type Item as follows,

```
Item *ptr;
```

- ✓ Object pointers are useful in creating object at run time. We can also use an object pointer to access the public members of an object.
- ✓ Consider the class Item defined as follows :

```
class Item
{
        int code;
        float price;
        public :
                void  getdata(int a , float b)
                {
                        code = a;
                        price = b;
                }
                void show(void)
                {
                        cout<<" Code : " << code << "\n";
                        cout<<" Price : " << price << "\n \n ";
                }
}
```

- ✓ Now declare the object of class Item as x and pointer for the object x as ptr.

```
Item x;
Item *ptr = &x;
```

- ✓ We can access the member function of Item in two ways, one by using the dot (.) operator and the object, and another by using the arrow operator and the object pointer.

```
x.getdata(10,20.5);
x.show( );
```

- ✓ These statements are equivalent to

```
X → getdata(10,20.5);
X → show( );
```

- ✓ Since *ptr is an alias of x, we can also use the following methods :

```
(*ptr) . show( );
```

- ✓ The parentheses are necessary because the dot operator has higher procedure than the indirection operator *.
- ✓ The need for using pointer to objects becomes clear when objects are to be created while the program is being executed, while is an instance of dynamic allocation of memory.
- ✓ We can also create the object using pointers and new operator as follows :

  Item *ptr = new Item;

- ✓ This statement allocates enough memory for the data members in the object structure and assigns the address of the memory space to ptr.
- ✓ Then ptr can be used to refer to the members as shown below:

  ptr → show( );

- ✓ We can also create an array of objects using pointers. For example, the statement

  Item *ptr = new Item[10];

- ✓ Remember, in such cases, if the class contains constructors, it must also contain an empty constructor.

Example :

```
// Pointer to object
#include<conio.h>
#include<iostream.h>
class Item
{
        // public :
                int no;
                int price;
          public :
                void get( int a, int p)
                {
                        no = a;
                        price = p;
                }
                void display( )
                {
                        cout<<"\n\n\n No := " <<no;
                        cout<<"\n\n Price := "<<price;
                }
};

int main( )
```

```
{
        clrscr( );
        int size = 3;
        //Item t[3];
        // Item *p = t;
         Item  *p = new Item[size];
         Item *q = p;
         int n,pr;
         for(int i=0; i<size; i++)
        {
                cout<<"\n Enter item no :";
                cin>>n;
                cout<<"\n Enter item price :";
                cin>>pr;
                p → get(n,pr);
                p++;
        }
                // p = &t[0];
        for(i=0; i<size; i++)
        {
                q → display( );
                q++;
                /* p→display( );
                   p++; */
        }
        getch( );
        return 0;
        }
}
```

Array of pointers to objects :

- ✓ In program we created space dynamically for three objects of equal size.
- ✓ But this may not be the case always. For example, the objects of a class that contains character string would not be of the same size.
- ✓ In such cases, we can define an array of pointers to objects that can be used to access the individual objects.

Example :

```
#include<conio.h>
#include<iostream.h>
#include<string.h>

class Stud
{
```

```
        int no;
        char *name;


                public :
                void get_stud( )
                {
                        char nm[50];
                        int len;
                        cout<<"\n Enter no:";
                        cin>>no;
                        cout<<"\n Enter name :";
                        cin>>nm;
                        int len = strlen(nm);
                        name = new char[len+1];
                        strcpy(name,nm);
                }
                void put_stud( )
                {
                        cout<<"\n No :"<<no;
                        cout<<"\n Name :"<<name;
                }
};
int main( )
{
        clrscr( );
        int const n=3;
        Stud *s[n];
        // s = new stud[n];
        int I = 0;
        char ch;
        do
        {
                s[i] = new stud;
                s[i] → get_stud( );
                // s[i] → put_stud( );
                cout<<"\n \n Do you want to  add more records ? (y/n) ";
                cin>>ch;
                i++;
        }while (ch == 'y' && i<n);
        if(i==n)
        {
                cout<<"\n Array index out of bound. . . . ";
        }
        for(int j=0; j<I; j++)
        {
```

```
        s[j] → put_stud( );
    }
    getch( );
    return 0;   }
```

This pointer :

- ✓ The keyword this identifies a special type of pointer.
- ✓ Suppose that you create an object named x of class A, and class A has a non static member function f( );
- ✓ If you call the function x.f( ), the keyword this in the body of f( ) stores the address of x. You can not declare this pointer or make assignments to it.
- ✓ This pointer points to the object for which the member function is called.
- ✓ Consider the following simple example :

```
class ABC
{
        int a;
        . . . . . . .
        . . . . . . .
};
```

- ✓ The private variable 'a' can be used directly inside a member function, like

```
        a = 123;
```

- ✓ We can also use the following statement to do the same job :

```
        this → a = 123;
```

- ✓ Since C++ permits the use of shorthand form a = 123, we have not been using the pointer this explicitly so far.
- ✓ However, we have been implicitly using the pointer this when overloading the operators using member function.
- ✓ Recall that, when a binary operator is overloading using a member function, we pass only one argument to the function.
- ✓ The other argument is implicitly passed using the pointer this. One important application of the pointer this is to return the object it points to.
- ✓ For example, the statement

```
        return *this;
```

- ✓ Inside a member function will return the object that invoked the function.
- ✓ This statement assumes important when we want to compare two or more objects inside a member function and return the invoking object as a result.

Example :

```
person &  person :: greater(person &x)
{
```

```
        if (x.age > age)
                return x;       // argument object
        else
                return *this; // invoking object
}
```

- ✓ Suppose we invoke this function by call

  max = A.greater(B);
- ✓ The function will return the object B if the age of the person B is greater than that of A, otherwise, it will return the object A using the pointer this.

Important notes on this pointer :

- ✓ This pointer stores the address of the class instance, to enable pointer access of the member to the member functions of the class.
- ✓ This pointer is not counted for calculated the size of the object.
- ✓ This pointers are not accessible for static member functions.

Example :

```
#include<conio.h>
#include<iostream.h>

class Max
{
        int val;

                public :
                void get( )
                {
                cout<< "\n Enter value :";
                cin>> this → val;
                }
                void put( )
                {
                        cout<<"\n Val : "<< this → val;
                }
                Max compare(Max m)
                {
                        if(val<m.val)
                                return m;
                        else
                                return *this;
                }
};

int main( )
```

```
{
        clrscr( );
        Max a,b,c;
        a.get( );
        b.get( );
        c = a.compare(b);
        c.put( );
        getch( );
        return 0;
}
```

Pointer to derived class :

- ✓ We can also use pointers for the objects of derived class.
- ✓ Pointers to objects of a base class are type – compatible with pointers to object of a derived class.
- ✓ Therefore, a single pointer variable can be made to point to objects belonging to different classes.
- ✓ For example, if B is a base class and D is a derived class from B, then a pointer declared as a pointer to B can also be a pointer to D.

Consider the following example :

```
B *cptr;      //pointer to class B type variable
B b;          // base object
D d;          // derived object
Cptr = &b;    // cptr points to object b
```

- ✓ Now we can make cptr to point to the object d as follows:

  ```
  Cptr = &d;  // cptr points to object d
  ```
- ✓ This is perfectly valid with C++ because d is an object derived from the class B.
- ✓ However, there is a problem in using cptr to access the public members of the derived class D.
- ✓ Using cptr, we can access only those members which are inherited from B and, not the members that originally belong to D.
- ✓ If in case a member of class D has the same name as the member of B, then any reference to that member by cptr will always access the base class member.
- ✓ Although C++ permits a base pointer to point to any object derived from that base, the pointer can not be directly used to access all the members of the derived class.
- ✓ We may have to use another pointer declared as pointer to the derived class type.

  Example :

  ```
  #include<conio.h>
  ```

```
#include<iostream.h>

class Base
{
        int a;
        public :
                void get_base( )
                {
                        cout<<"\n Enter a :";
                        cin>>a;
                }
                void put( )
                {
                        cout<<"\n A: "<<a
                }
};

class Derived : public Base
{
        int b;
        public :
                void get_der( )
                {
                        cout<<"\n Enter b :";
                        cin>>b;
                }
                void put_der( )
                {
                        cout<<"\n B: "<<b;
                }
};


int main( )
{
        clrscr( );
        Base b, *bp;
        bp = &b;
        bp → get_base( );
        bp → put( );

        Derived d,*dp;
        bp = &d;
        bp → get_base( )
        bp → put( );
```

```
    /* bp → get_der( );
    bp → put_der( );   not allowed as these are member of derived
class */

    cout<<"Using ((derived *)bp)\n";
    (( derived *)bp) → get_der( );          // cast bp to derived type
    (( derived *)bp) → put( );         // cast bp to derived type
    dp = &d;
    dp → get_base( );
    dp → base :: put( );
    dp → get_der( );

    dp → put_der( );
    getch( );
    return 0;
}
```

- ✓ We have used the statement

  bp → put( );
- ✓ Two times. First when bp points to the base object, and the second when bp points to derived object.
- ✓ But, both the times, it executed base :: put( ) function and displayed the content of the base object.
- ✓ However the statements

  dp → put_der( );

  ((derived *) bp) → put( );   // cast bp to derived type
- ✓ Display the contents of the derived object. This shows that although a base pointer can be made to point to any of derived objects, it cannot directly access the members defined by a derived class.

8.3 Virtual Function :

- ✓ An essential requirement of polymorphism the ability to refer to objects without any regard to their classes.
- ✓ This requirement can be achieved by the use of a single pointer variable to refer to the objects of different classes. Here, we use the pointer to base class to refer to all the derived objects.
- ✓ But, we just discovered that a base pointer, even when it is made to contain the address of a derived class, always executes the function in the base class.
- ✓ Compiler simply ignores the contents of the pointer and chooses the member function that matches the type of the pointer.
- ✓ How do we then achieve polymorphism? It is achieved using what is known as 'virtual' function.
- ✓ A virtual function is a member function that is declared within a base class and redefined by a derived class.

- ✓ When a class containing a virtual function is inherited, the derived class redefines the virtual function to fit its own needs.
- ✓ The virtual function within the base class defines the form of the interface to that function.
- ✓ Each redefinition of the virtual function by a derived class implements its operation as it relates specifically to the derived class. That is, the redefinition creates a specific method.
- ✓ Normally virtual function behaves just like any other type of class member function.
- ✓ But, we can achieve run time polymorphism via virtual function when we access it through the pointer.
- ✓ When we use the same function name in both the base and derived classes, the function in base class is declared as virtual using the keyboard virtual preceding its normal declaration.
- ✓ When a function is made virtual, C++ determine which function to use at run time based on the type of object pointed to by the base pointer, rather than the type of the pointer.
- ✓ Thus, by making the base pointer to point to different objects, we can execute different version of the virtual function.

Example :

```
#include<iostream.h>
#include<conio.h>

class Base
{
        public : virtual void display( )
                {
                        cout<<"\n Base display…";
                }
};

class Derived1 : public Base
{
        public : void display( )
                {
                        cout<<"\n Derived1 display…..";
                }
};
class Derived2 : public Base
{
        public : void display( )
                {
                        cout<<"\n Derived2 display…..";
                }
};
```

```
int main( )
{
        clrscr( );
        Base b,*p;
        Derived1 d1;
        Derived2 d2;

        P = &b;
        P → display( );

        // base reference
        Base &q1 = d1;
        q1.display( );

        P = &d1;
        P → display( );

        p = &d2;
        p → display( );

        // base reference
        Base &q2 = d2;
        q2.display( );

        getch( );
        return 0;
}
```

- ✓ One important point to remember is that, we must access virtual functions through the use of a pointer declared as pointer to the base class.
- ✓ Why can't we use the object name the ame way as any other member function to call the virtual function?
- ✓ We can, but remember, run time polymorphism is achieved only when a virtual function is accessed through a pointer to the base class.

Rules for virtual function:

- ✓ When virtual functions are created for implementing late binding, we should follow some rules that satisfy the compiler requirements.
- ✓ The virtual function must be members of some class.
- ✓ They cannot be static.
- ✓ They are accessed by using object pointers.
- ✓ A virtual function can be a friend of another class.
- ✓ A virtual function in a base class must be defined, even though it may not be used.

- ✓ The prototypes of the base class version of a virtual function and all the derived class versions must be identical. If two functions with the same name have different prototypes C++ considers them as overloaded functions, and the virtual function mechanism is ignored.
- ✓ We cannot have virtual constructors, but we can have virtual destructors.
- ✓ While a base pointer can point to any type of the derived object, the reverse is not true. That is to say, we cannot use a pointer to a derived class to access an object of the base type.
- ✓ When a base pointer points to a derived class, incrementing or decrementing it will not make it to point to the next object of the derived class. It is incremented or decremented only relative to its base type. Therefore, we should not use this method to move the pointer to the next object.
- ✓ If virtual function is defined in the base class, it need not be necessarily redefined in the derived class. In such cases, calls will invoke the base function.

Pure Virtual Function:

- ✓ It is normal practice to declare a function virtual inside the base class and redefined it in the derived classes.
- ✓ The function inside the base class is seldom used for performing any task. It only serves as a placeholder.

For example, we have defined the class base as follows :

```
class base
{
        public : virtual void display( );
};
```

- ✓ Here display( ) function does not contain function body it means it has empty body and we are not defining any object of class base then such functions are called "do nothing" functions.
- ✓ A "do nothing" function may be defined as follows :

```
virtual void display( ) = 0;
```

- ✓ Such functions are called pure virtual function. A pure virtual function is a function declared in a base class that has no definition relative to the base class.
- ✓ In such cases, the compiler requires each derived class to either define the function or redeclare it as a pure virtual function.
- ✓ Remember that a class containing pure virtual function cannot be used to declare any objects of its own.
- ✓ Such classes are called abstract base classes. The main objective of an abstract base class is to provide some traits to the derived classes and to create a base pointer required for achieving run time polymorphism.

UNIT – 9
Console I/O Operations

Every program takes some data as input and generates processed data as output following the familiar input output cycle.

9.1 C++ Streams :

- The I/O system in C++ is designed to work with a wide variety of devices including terminals, disks, and tape drives. Although each device is very different, the I/O system supplies an interface to the programmer that is independent of the actual device being accessed. This interface is known as stream.
- A stream is a sequence of bytes. It acts either as source from which the input data can be obtained or as a destination to which the output data can be sent.
- The source stream that provides data to the program is called the input stream and the destination stream that receives output from the program is called the output stream.
- In other words a program extracts the bytes from an input stream and inserts bytes into an output stream as illustrated in following figure.

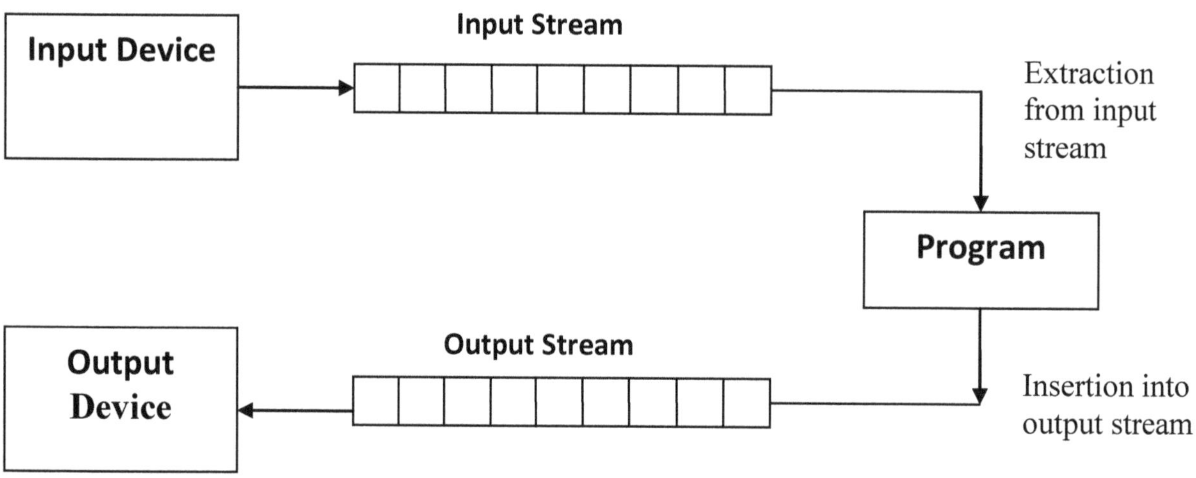

Figure :- Data Stream

- The data in the input stream can come from the keyboard or any other storage devices. Similarly, the data in the output stream can go to the screen or any other storage device.
- A stream acts as an interface between the program and the input/output device. Therefore a C++ program handles data input or output independent of the devices used.

C++ Stream Classes :

- The C++ I/O system contains a hierarchy of classes that are used to define various streams to deal with both the console and disk files. These are called stream classes.

- Following figure shows hierarchy of the stream classes used for input and output operations with the console units. These classes are declared in the header file iostream.h. This file should be included in all the programs that communicate with the console unit.
- The **ios** is the base class for istream (input stream) and ostream (output stream) which are, in turn, base classes for iostream(input/output stream). The class ios is declared as virtual base class so that only one copy of its members are inherited by the iostream.

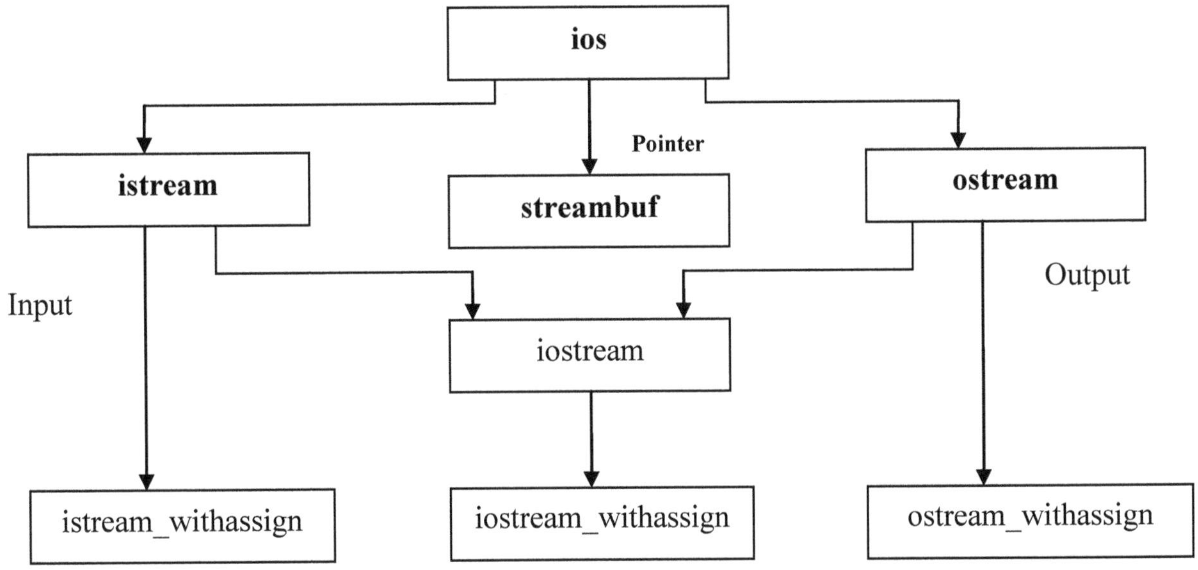

Stream classes for console operations :

Class name	*Contents*
ios (General input/output stream class)	Used by all other input output classes
istream (input stream)	Inherits the properties of ios Declare functions such as get( ),getline ( ) and read() Contains overloaded extraction operator >>
ostream (output stream)	Inherits the properties of ios Declare functions such as put( ) and write ( ) Contains overloaded insertion operaror <<
iostream (input/output stream)	Inherits the properties of ios, istream and ostream classes through multiple inheritance and thus contains all the input and output functions.
Streambuf	Provides an interface to physical devices through buffers

9.2 Unformatted and formatted I/O operations :
Overloaded operators >> and <<

- We have used the objects **cin** and **cout** predefined in the iostream file for the input and output of data of various type.
- This has been made by overloading the operators >> and << to recognize the basic C++ data types. The >> operator is overloaded in the istream class and << is overloaded in the ostream class. The following format for reading data from the keyboard is used:

  cin >> variable1 >> variable2 >> variable3 … … >> variable N
- This statement will cause the computer to stop the execution and look for input data from the keyboard. The input data should be separated by white spaces and should match the type of variable in the **cin** list. Spaces and new line and tabs will be skipped.

- The operator >> reads the data character by character and assigns it to the indicated location. The reading for a variable will be terminated at the encounter of a white space or a character that does not match the destination type.
- The general form for displaying data on the screen is:

  cout << item1 << iem2 << item3 << … … << itemN

  The item1 through itemN may be variables or constants of any basic type.

Example :

```
int code;
cin >> code;
cout << code;
```

put( ) and get( ) functions :

- The classes istream and ostream define two functions get( ) and put respectively to handle the single character input / output operations.
- There are two type of get( ) functions. We can use both get(char *) and get(void) prototypes to fetch a character including the blank space and tab and the new line character.
- The getchar (char *) version assign the input character to its argument and the get(void) version returns the input character.

Example of get():

```
#include <iostream.h>
int main ()
{
        char c, str[256];
        cout << "Enter the name ";
        cin.get (str,20); // read only frist 19 char + 1 char null
        cout<<str;
        return 0;
}
```

Example of put():

```
#include <iostream.h>
```

```
int main()
{
        int count = 0;
        char c;
        cout << "INPUT TEXT\n";
        cin.get(c);
        whi1e(c != '\n')
        {
                cout.put(c);
                count++;
                cin.get(c);
        }
        cout << "\nNumber of characters = " << count << "\n";
        return O;
}
Input
Object Oriented Programming
Output
Object Oriented Programming
Number of characters = 27
```

getline() and write( ) functions :

- We can read and display a line of text more efficiently by using the lien-oriented input/output functions getline( ) and write( ) function.
- The getline ( ) function reads a whole line of text that ends with a new line character transmitted by the RETURN key. This function can be invoked by using the object **cin** as follows.
  cin.getline (line, size);
- The write function display an entire line and has the following form :
  cout.write(line, size);

Example of getline() & write():

```
#include <iostream.h>
int main()
{
        char name[25];
        cin.getline(name, 20);          // read only frist 19 char + 1
char null
        cout.write(name, 25);
                //print 25 char string, if less than 24 char then print
garbage char.
}
```

Formatted Console I/O Operations and Manipulators :

C++ supports a number of features that could be used for formatting the output. These features include :

1) ios class function and flags.

2) ***Manipulators.***
3) ***User - Defined output functions.***

The ios class contains a large number of member function that would help us to format the output in a number of ways. The most important once among them are listed below.

Function	Task
width( )	To Specify required field size for displaying an output value.
precision( )	To specify the number of digits to be displayed after decimal point of a float value.
fill( )	To specify a character that is used to fill the unused portion of a field.
setf( )	To specify format flags that can control the form of output display as left or right justification.
unsetf( )	To clear the flags specified.

Example:

```
#include <iostream.h>
#include <iomanip.h>
int main()
{
   const float tenth = 0.1;
   const float one   = 1.0;
   const float big   = 1234567890.0;
   cout << tenth << ", " << one << ", " << big << endl;
   cout.precision(3);
   cout  << tenth << ", " << one << ", " << big << endl;
   cout.setf(ios::left,ios::adjustfield);
   cout.fill("*");
   cout.width(8);
   cout <<"abc"<<endl;
   cout.precision(20);
   cout  << tenth << endl;
   cout.width(8);
   cout.fill('*');
   cout << 34 << 45 << endl;
   cout.width(8);
   cout << 34 ;
   cout.width(8);
   cout << 45 << endl;
   return 0;
}
Output:
0.1, 1, 1.234578e+09
```

```
0.1, 1, 1.235e+09
abc*****
0.1000000014901161193 8
34******45
34******45******
```

9.3 Manipulators :

- Manipulators are special functions that can be included in the I/O statements to alter the format parameters of a stream.
- Following table shows some important manipulators functions that are frequently used. To access manipulators, the file ***iomanip.h*** should be included in the program.

Manipulator	**Equivalent ios function**
setw( )	width ( )
setprecision ( )	precision ( )
setfill ( )	fill ( )
setiosflags ( )	setf ( )
resetiosflags	unsetf ( )

Defining Field Width : width()

- We can use wdith() function to define the width of a field necessary for the output of an item. Since, it si a member function, we have to use an object to invoke it, as shown below:

  cout.width(w);

- where **w** is the field width (number of column). The output will be printed in a field of **w** characters wide at the right end of the field. The width() function can specify the field width for only one item(The item that follows immediately). After printing one item (as per the specification) it will revert back to the default. For example, the statements:

  cout.width(5);
  cout << 543 << 12 <<"\n";

  will produce following output:

		5	4	3	1	2

- The value 543 is printed right-justified in the first five columns. The specification width(5) does not retain the setting for the printing the number 12. This can be improved as follows:

  cout.width(5);
  cout << 543;
  cout.width(5)
  cout << 12 << "\n";

  This produce the following output :

		5	4	3				1	2

- Remember that the field width should be specified for each item separately. C++ never truncates the values and therefore, if the specified width is smaller than the size of the value to be printed, C++ expand the field to fit the value.

Example :

```
#include <iostream.h>
#include <conio.h>
int main()
{
        clrscr();
        int item[4] = {10,8,12,15};
        int cost[4] = {75,100,60,99};
        cout.width(5);
        cout<<"ITEMS";
        cout.width(8);
        cout<<"COST";
        cout.width(15);
        cout<<"TOTAL VALUE \n";
        int sum =0;
        for(int i=0;i<4;i++)
        {
                cout.width(5);
                cout<<item[i];
                cout.width(8);
                cout<<cost[i];
                int value = item[i]*cost[i];
                cout.width(15);
                cout<<value<<"\n";
                sum=sum +value;
        }
        cout<<"\n Grand Total = ";
        cout.width(2);
        cout<<sum<<"\n";
        getch();
        return 0;
}
```

Output :

```
ITEMS          COST        TOTAL VALUE
10        75         750
8         100        800
12        60         720
15        99         1485

Grand Total = 3755
```

Setting Precision: precision()

- By default, the floating numbers are printed with six digits after the decimal points. However, we can specify the number of digits to be displayed after the decimal point while printing the floating point numbers.
- This can be done by using the precision( ) member function as follows:

  cout.precision(d);

  where **d** is the number of digits to be right of the decimal points. For Example, the statements

```
cout.precision(3);
cout << sqrt(2) <<"\n";
cout << 3.14159 <<"\n";
cout << 2.50032 << "\n";
```

  will produce the following output:

```
1.141      (truncated)
2.142      (rounded to the nearest cent)
2.5        (no trailing zero)
```

- Note that, unlike the function width(), precision() retains the setting in effect until it is reset.
- We can set different values to different precision as follows:

```
cout.precesion(3);
cout << sqrt(2);
cout.precesion(5);        //Reset the precision
cout << 3.14159 << "\n"
Example :
#include <iostream.h>
#include <conio.h>
#include <math.h>
int main()
{
        cout<<"precesion set to 2 digits \n\n";
        cout.precesion(2);
        cout.width(10);
        cout<<"VALUE";
        cout.width(15);
        cout<<"SQRT OF VALUE"<<"\n";
        for(int i=1;i<5;i++)
```

```
    {
        cout.width(8);
        cout<<i;
        cout.width(13);
        cout<<sqrt(i)<<"\n";
    }
    cout<<"\n Precesion set to 5 digits \n\n";
    cout.precesion(5);
    cout<<"sqrt(10) ="<<sqrt(10)<<"\n\n";
    cout.precesion(0);              //precesion set to default
    cout<<"sqrt(10) ="<<sqrt(10)<<"default setting\n";
    getch();
    return 0;
}
```

```
Precesion set to 3 digits
      VALUE            SQRT OF VALUE
        1              1
        2              1.41
        3              1.73
        4              2
        5              2.24
Precesion set to 5 digits
sqrt(10) = 3.16238
sqrt(10) = 3.162278     default setting
```

Filling and Padding : fill()

- We have been printing the values using much larger field widths than required by the values.
- The unused position of the field is filled with white spaces, by default. However, we can use the fill function to fill the unused positions by any desired character. It is used in the following form.

  cout.fill(ch);

  Where, ch represents the character which is used for filling the unused positions.

  Example:

  ```
  cout.fill('*');
  cout.width(10);
  cout << 5250 << "\n";
  ```

  The output would be:

*	*	*	*	*	*	5	2	5	0

- Financial institutions and banks use this kind of padding while printing cheques so that no one can change the amount easily. Like precesion(), fill() stays in effect till we change it.

  Example :

```
#include <iostream.h>
#include <conio.h>
#include <iomanip.h>
int main()
{
        cout.fill('*');
        cout.width(15);
        cout.precision(3);
        cout<<12.3456;
        getch();
        return 0;
}
Output :
*********12.346
```

Formatting Flags, Bit-fields and setf() :

- We have seen that when the function width() is used, the value(whether text or number) is printed right-justified in the field width created. But, it is a usual practice to print the text left-justified. How do we get a value printed left-justified? Or, how do we get a floating point number in the scientific notation?
- The setf(), a member function of the ios class, can provide answers to these and many other formatting questions. The setf() (setf stans for set flags) function can be used as follows:

  cout.setf(arg1,arg2);
- The arg1 is one of the formatting flags defined in the class ios. The formatting flag specifies the format action required for the output. Anouhter, ios constant, agr2, known as bit field specifies the group to which the formatting flag belongs.
- Following table the bit field, flag and their format action. There are three bit fields and each has a group of format flags.

Table : Flags and bit field of setf() function

Format required	*Flag (arg1)*	*Bit-field (arg2)*
Left-justified output	ios :: left	ios :: adjustfield
Right-justified output	ios :: right	ios :: adjustfield
Padding after sign or base Indicator (like +##20)	ios :: internal	ios :: adjustfield
Scientific notation	ios :: scientific	ios :: floatfield
Fixed point notation	ios :: fixed	ios :: floatfield
Decimal base	ios :: dec	ios :: basefield
Octal base	ios :: oct	ios :: basefield
Hexadecimal base	ios :: hex	ios :: basefield

Example :

```
cout.fill('*');
cout.setf(ios :: left, ios :: adjustfield );
cout.width(15);
cout<<"ATMIYA" <<"\n";
```

This will produce the following output :

A	T	M	I	Y	A	*	*	*	*	*	*	*	*	*

Designing Our Own Manipulators

We can design our own manipulators for certain special purposes. The general form for creating a manipulator without any arguments is:

```
ostream & manipulator (ostream & output)
{
   .....
   .....  (code)
   .....
   return output;
}
```

Here, the *manipulator* is the name of the manipulator under creation. The following function defines a manipulator called **unit** that displays "inches":

```
ostream & unit(ostream & output)
{
       output << " inches";
       return output;
}
```

The statement

```
cout << 36 << unit;
```

will produce the following output

```
36 inches
```

We can also create manipulators that could represent a sequence of operations. Example:

```
ostream & show(ostream & output)
{
        output.setf(ios::showpoint);
        output.setf(ios::showpos);
        output << setw(10);
        return output;
}
```

This function defines a manipulator called **show** that turns on the flags **showpoint** and **showpos** declared in the class **ios** and sets the field width to 10.

Program 10.9 illustrates the creation and use of the user-defined manipulators. The program creates two manipulators called **currency** and **form** which are used in the **main**

Example:

```
#include <iostream>
#include <iomanip>

using namespace std;

// user-defined manipulators

ostream & currency(ostream & output)
{
        output << "Rs";
        return output;
}

ostream & form(ostream & output)
{
        output.setf(ios::showpos);
        output.setf(ios::showpoint);
```

```
        output.fill('*');
        output.precision(2);
        output << setiosflags(ios::fixed)
               << setw(10);
        return output;
}

int main()
{
        cout << currency << form << 7864.5;

        return 0;
}
```

The output of Program 10.9 would be:

```
Rs**+7864.50
```

UNIT - 10
Working with files

- Many real-life problems handle large volumes of data and in such situations we need to use some devices such as floppy disks or hard disk to store the data.
- The data is stored in these devices using the concept of files. A file is a collection of related data stored in a particular area on the disk.
- Programs can be designed to perform the read and write operations on these files.
- A program typically involves either or both of the following kinds of data communication:
    1. ***Data transfer between the console unit and the program.***
    2. ***Data transfer between the program and a disk file.***
- The I/O system of C++ handles file operations which are very much similar to the console input and output operations.
- It uses file streams as an interface between the programs and files.
- The stream that supplies data to the program is known as input stream and the one receives data from the program is known as output stream.

- In other words, the input stream extracts or reads data from the file and the output stream inserts or writes data to the file. This is illustrated in following figure.
- The input operation involves the creation of an input stream and linking it with the program and the input file. Similarly the output operation involves establishing an output stream with the necessary links with the program and the output files.

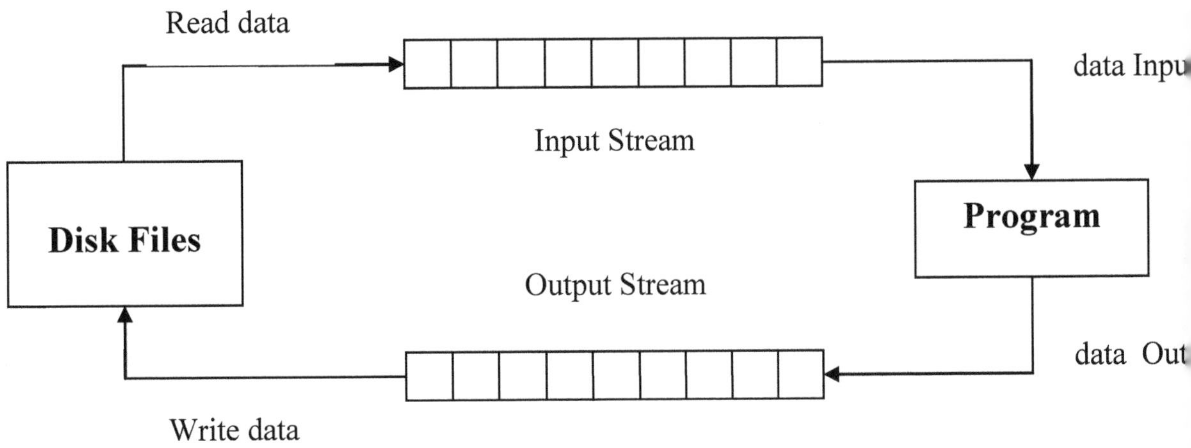

File Input and Output Stream

10.1 File stream classes :

The I/O system of C++ contains a set of classes that define the file handling methods. These include ifstream, ofstream and fstream. These classes are derived from fstreambase and from the corresponding iostream class as shown in following hierarchy. These classes are designed to manage the disk files, are declared in fstream and therefore we must include this file in any program that uses files.

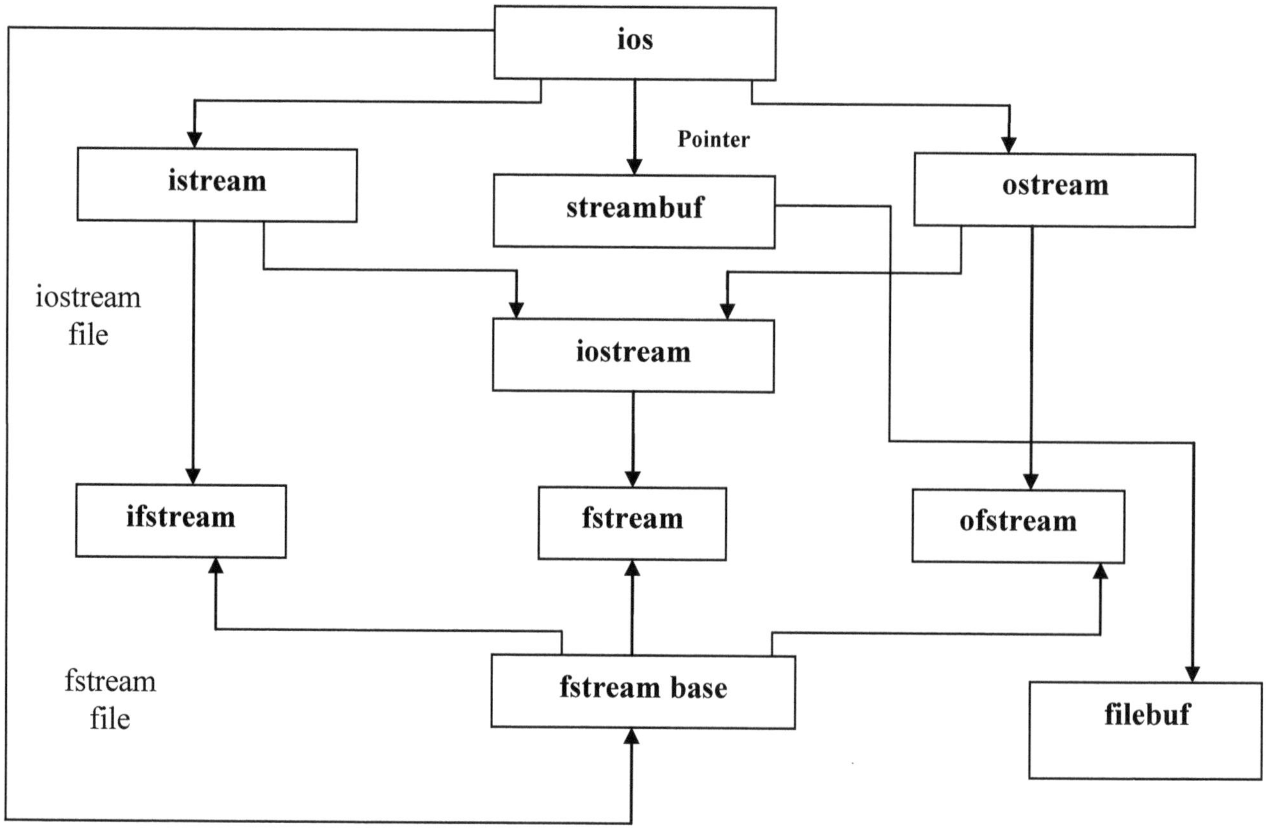

Stream classes for file operations contained in fstream file

Following table shows the details of file stream classes. Note that these classes contains many more features.

Class	Contents
filebuf	Set the file buffer to read and write. Contains Openprot constant used in open( ) of file stream classes. Also contains close( ) and open( ) as members.
fstreambase	Provides common file stream operations. Serves a base for fstream, ifstream and ofstream class. Contains open( ) and close( ) functions.
ifstream	Provides input operations. Contains open with default input mode. Inherits the function get( ), getline( ), read( ), seekg( ), and tellg( ) functions from istream.
ofstream	Provides output operations. Contains open ( ) with default mode. Inherits put() , seekp( ). tellp( ), and write( ) functions from ostream.
fstream	Provides supports for simultaneous input and output operations. Contains open( ) with default input mode. Inherits all the function from istream and ostream classes through iostream.

Opening and Closing a file :

- If we want to use a disk file we, need to decide the following things about the file and its intended use.
  1. ***Suitable name for the file***
  2. ***Data type and structure.***

3. ***Purpose.***
4. ***Opening method.***

- The filename is a string of characters that make up a valid filename for the operating system. It may contain two parts, a primary name and an optional period with extension.
- We must first create a file stream and then link it to the filename. A file stream can be defined using the classes ifstream , ofstream and fstream that are contained in the header file ***fstream.***
- The class to be used depends upon the purpose that is, whether we want to read data from the file or write data to it. A file can be opened in two ways.
  1. ***Using the constructor function of the class.***
  2. ***Using the member function open () of the class.***
- The first method is useful when we use only one file in the stream. The second method is used when we want to manage multiple files using one stream.

Opening Files Using Constructor :

- We know that a constructor is used to initialize an object while it is being created. Here, a filename is used to initialize the file stream object. This involves the following steps.
  1) *Create a file stream object to manage the stream using the appropriate class. That is to say the class ofstream is used to create the output stream and the class ifstream to create the input stream.*
  2) *Initialize the file object with the desired filename.*
- For example following statement opens a file named "results" for output.

```
ostream outfile("results");
```

- Similarly the following statement declares infile as an ifstream object and attaches it to the file data for reading or input.

```
ifstream infile("data");
```

Example reading writing using infile and outfile.

```
outfile << "Total";
outfile << sum;
infile >> number;
infile >> string;
```

- Every file that has been opened must be closed when no further necessary. To close a file following statement is used.

```
outfile.close( );
infile.close ( );
```

Above statements disconnects the file from the output stream and input stream. Remember, the objects infile and outfile are still exist and files may again be connected to outfile or infile objects.

Example:

```
# include <iostream.h>
#include <fstream.h>
```

```
void main()
{
        ofstream outfile("sample.txt");                    // create file for
  output
        char ch = 'a';
         int i = 12;
        float f = 4356.15;
        char arr[ ] = "hello";
        outfile << ch << endl <<< i <<endl<< f << endl << arr;
  //send the data to file
        outfile.close();
        ifstream infile("sample.txt");
        ch=' ' ;
        i=0;
        f=0;
        infile >> ch >> i >> f>> arr;                         // read data
  from file
        cout << ch<<endl << i<<endl << f << arr;              // send data
  to screen
  }
```

Opening a file using open ( ) :

As, the function open( ) can be used to open multiple files that use the same stream object. For example, we may want to process a set of file sequentially. In such cases we may create a single stream object and use it to open each file in turn. This is done as follows.

```
File-stream-class stream-object;
Stream-object.open("filename");
ofstream outfile;
outfile.open("DATA1");
... ...
... ...
outfile.close( );
outfile.open("DATA2");
... ...
... ...
outfile.close( );
```

Example:

```
#include<iostream.h>
#include <fstream.h>
class person
{
        private:
        char name[40];
        int age;
        public:
        void getdata()
```

```
        {
                cout << "\n Enter name:"; cin >> name;
                cout << "\n Enter age:"; cin >> age;
        }
} ; // End of the class definition
void main()
{
        person per ;            // Define an object of person class
        per.getdata();                  // Enter the values to the data
members of the class.
        ofstream outfile;
        outfile.open("person.txt");          // Open the file in output mode
        outfile.write((char*)&per, sizeof(per));          // Write the object
into the file
}
```

Error Handling during file Operations :

- One of the following things may happen when dealing with the files:
    1. A file which we are attempting to open for reading does not exist.
    2. The file name used for a new file may already exist.
    3. We may attempt an invalid operation such as reading past the end-of-file.
    4. There may not be any space in the disk for storing more data
    5. We may use an invalid file name.
    6. We may attempt to perform an operation when the file is not opened for that purpose.
- The C++ file stream inherits a "stream-state" member form the class ios. This member records information on the status of a file in being used. The stream state member uses bit field to store the status of the error conditions stated above.
- The class ios supports several member functions that can be used to read the status recorded in a file stream. These functions along with their meanings are listed in following table.

Function	Return value and meaning
eof( )	Returns true if end-of-file is encountered while reading. Otherwise returns false.
fail( )	Returns true when an input or output operation is failed.
bad( )	Returns true if an invalid operation is attempted or any unrecoverable error has occurred. However if it is false, it may be possible to recover from any other error reported and continue operation.
good( )	Returns true if no error has occurred. This means all the above functions are false. For example if

	file.good( ) is true, all is well with the stream file and we can proceed to perform I/O operations. When it returns false, no further operations can be carried out.

Example:

```
#include <iostream.h>
#include <fstream.h>
#include <string.h>
int main ()
 {
  string line;
  ifstream myfile ("example.txt");
  if (myfile.good())
  {
     If(!myfile.bad())
    {
       while (! myfile.eof() )
           {
           getline (myfile,line);
           cout << line << endl;
           }
    }
    else
    {
     Cout<<"unable to read file";
    }
   myfile.close();
  }
  else
     cout << "Unable to open file";
  return 0;
 }
```

10.2 File Modes :

- The ***open*** function can take two arguments, one for a file name and second foe a file mode. The general form of the function open( ) with two argument is :

  Stream-object.open ("filename", mode);

- The second argument mode called file mode parameter specifies the purpose for which the file is opened. The second parameter uses the default values in the absence of the actual values. The default values are as follows.

ios :: in // for ifstream functions meaning open for reading only.

ios :: out // for ofstream functions meaning open for writing only.

- The file mode parameter can take one or more of such constants defined in the class ios. Following table lists the file mode parameters and their meanings.

Parameter	Meaning
ios :: app	Append to end-of-file
ios :: ate	Go to the end-of-file.
ios :: binary	Binary file
ios :: in	Open file for reading only
ios:: nocreate	Open fails if the file does not exist
ios :: noreplace	Open fails if the file already exists.
ios :: out	Open file for writing only
ios :: trunk	Delete the contents of the file if it exists.

Example:

```
#include<iostream.h>
#include<fstream.h>
#include<conio.h>
void main()
{
        clrscr();
        fstream out("D:\test.txt", ios::app | ios::in | ios::out);
        ifstream in("D:\temp.txt");
        char ch;
        while(in)
        {
                in.get(ch);
                cout << ch;
        }
        while(out)
        {
                out.get(ch);
                cout << ch;
        }
        getch();
}
```

Rereading a complete binary file :

```
#include <iostream.h>
#include <fstream.h>
ifstream::pos_type size;
```

```
char * memblock;

int main ()
{
 ifstream file ("example.bin", ios::in|ios::binary|ios::ate);
 if (file.is_open())
 {
  size = file.tellg();
  memblock = new char [size];
  file.seekg (0, ios::beg);
  file.read (memblock, size);
  file.close();
  cout << "the complete file content is in memory";
  delete[] memblock;
 }
 else cout << "Unable to open file";
 return 0;
}
```

File Pointers:

- Each file has two associated pointers known as the file pointers. One of them is called the input pointer or get pointer and the other is called the output pointer or put pointer.
- We can use these pointers to move through the file while reading or writing.
- The input pointer is used for reading the contents of a given file location and the output pointer is used for writing to a given file location. Each time an input or output operation takes place, the appropriate pointer is automatically advanced.
- **Function for manipulating of File Pointers**

seekg( )	Moves get pointer (input) to a specified location.
seekp( )	Moves put pointer (output) to a specified location.
tellg( )	Gives the current position of the get pointer.
tellp( )	Gives the current position of the put pointer.

```
seekg (offset , refposition);
seekp(offset, refposition);
```

- The parameter offset represents the number of bytes the file pointer is to be moved from the location specified by the parameter refposition. The refposition takes one of the following three constants defined in the ios class:

ios :: beg	start of the file
ios :: cur	current position of the pointer
ios :: end	End of file

Example:

```
#include <iostream.h>
#include <fstream.h>
int main ()
 {
    long begin,end;
    ifstream myfile ("example.txt");
    begin = myfile.tellg();
    myfile.seekg (0, ios::end);
    end = myfile.tellg();
    myfile.close();
    cout << "size is: " << (end-begin) << " bytes.\n";
    return 0;
 }
```

Sequential Input and Output Operations:

- Reading and writing sequentially in files, C++ offers several member functions in a file stream classes.
- The functions put( ) and get( ) are designed for handling a single character at a time. Similarly write ( ) and read( ) handle the data in binary form. This means that the values are stored in the disk file in the same format in which they are stored in memory. It is possible to write and read entire object of class using these functions. Only one important point is to remember is that only data are written to the disk file and the member functions are not.

10.3 Updating a file: Random Access

- Updating is a routine task in the maintenance of any data file. The updating would include one or more of the following tasks.
    1. ***Displaying the contents of a file.***
    2. ***Modifying an existing item.***
    3. ***Adding a new item.***
    4. ***Deleting an existing item.***
- These actions require the file pointers to move to a particular location that corresponds to the item/object under consideration. This can be easily implemented if the file contains a collection of items/objects of equal lengths. In such cases, the size of each object can be obtained using the statement

```
int object_length = sizeof(object);
```

- Then, the location of a desired object, say the mth object, may be obtained as follows:

```
int location = m * object_length;
```

- The location gives the byte number of the first byte of the mth object. Now, we can set the file pointer to reach this byte with the help of seekg() or seekp().

- We can also find out the total number of objects in a file using the object_length as
follows:
  int n = file_size/object_length;

- The file_size can be obtained using the function tellg() or tellp() when the file pointer is
located at the end of the file.
- Following Program illustrates how some of the tasks described above are carried out. The program uses the "STOCKDAT" file created using Program for five items and performs the following operations on the file:
  1. Adds a new item to the file.
  2. Modifies the details of an item.
  3. Displays the contents of the file.

```
#include <iostream.h>
#include <fstream.h>
#include <i omanip.h>
class INVENTORY
{
        char name[10];
        int code;
        float cost;
        pubiic:
        void getdata(void)
        {
                cout << "Enter name: "; Cin >> name;
                cout << "Enter code: "; cin >> code;
                cout << "Enter cost: "; cin >> cost;
        void putdata(void)
        {
                cout << setw(10) << name
                << setw(1O) << code
                << setprecision(2) << setw(1O) << cost
                << endi;
        }
}; // End of ciass definition
int main()
{
        INVENTORY item;
        fstream inoutfiie; // input/output stream
        inoutfi1e.open("STOCK.DAT", ios:: ate I ios:: in |
        ioszzout I ios::binary);
        inoutfiie.seekg(O,ios:zbeg); // go to start
        cout << "CURRENT CONTENTS OF STOCK" << "\n";
```

```
        whil e(inoutfil e.read((char *) & item, sizeof item))
        {
                item.putdata();
        }
        inoutfil e.ciear();           // turn of EOF flag
        /* >>>>>>>>>>>>>> Add one more item <<<<<<<<<<<<<<
        cout << "\nADD AN ITEM\n";
        item.getdata();
        char ch;
        cin.get(ch);
        inoutfiie.write((char *) & item, sizeof item);        // Display
    the appended file
        inoutfiie.seekg(0);           // go to the start
```

Command line arguments :

- Like C, C++ too supports a feature that facilitates the supply of argument to the main() function. These arguments are supplied at the time of invoking the program. They are typically used to pass the names of data file.

  Example

  C:\> exam data.txt results.txt
- Here, exam is the name of the file containing the program to be executed and data.txt and result.txt are the filenames passed to the program as command line arguments.
- The command-line arguments are typed by the user and are delimited by a space. The first argument is always the filename (command name) and contains the program to be executed. How do these arguments get into the program?
- The main() functions which we have been using up to now without any arguments can take two arguments as shown below:

  main(int argc, char * argv[])
- The first argument argc (known as argument counter) represents the number of arguments in the command line. The second argument argv (known as argument vector) is an array of char type pointers that points to the command line arguments. The size of this array will be equal to the value of argc. For instance, for the command line

  C > exam data results
- The value of argc would be 3 and the argv would be an array of three pointers to strings as
  shown below :

  argv[0] ---> exam
  argv[1] ---> data
  argv[2] ---> results .

- Note that argv[0] always represents the command name that invokes the program. The character pointers argv[1] and argv[2] can be used as file names in the file opening statements as shown below:

```
infile.open(argv[l]);          // open data file for reading
outfile.open(argv[2]);         // open results file for writing
```

- Program illustrates the use of the command-line arguments for supplying the file names. The command line is test ODD EVEN The program creates two files called ODD and EVEN using the command-line arguments, and a set of numbers stored in an array are written to these files. Note that the odd numbers are written to the file ODD and the even numbers are written to the file EVEN. The program then displays the contents of the files.

Example:

```
#include <iostream.h>
#include <fstream.h>
#inciude <stdlib.h>
int main(int argc, char * argv[])
{
        int number[9] = {11,22,33,44,55,66,77,88,99};
        if(argc != 3)
        {
                cout << "argc = " << argc << "\n";
                cout << "Error in arguments \n";
                exit(1);
        }
        ofstream foutl, fout2;
        fout1.open(argv[1]);
        if(fout1.fai1())
        {
                cout << "cou1d not open the fi1e"<< argv[1] << "\n";
                exit(1);
        }
        fout2.open(argv[2]);
        if(f<>ur2.fa11 ())
        {
                cout << "could not open the fi1e "<< argv[2] << "\n";
                exit(1);
        }
        for(int i=0; 1<9; i++)
        {
                if(number[i] % 2 == 0)
                        fout2 << number[i] << " ' // write to EVEN file
                else
                        foutl << number[i] << " ' // write to ODD file
        }
```

```
        fout1.close();
        fout2.c1ose();
        ifstream fin;
        char ch;
        for(i=1; i<argc; i++)
                fin.open(argv[i]);» s
        cout << "Contents of " << argv[i] << "\n“;
        do
        {
                fin.get(ch);            // read a value
                cout << ch; // display it
                }while(fin);
                cout << "\n\n";
                fin.close();
                return 0;
}
```

The output of Program would be:

Contents of ODD

11 33 55 77 99

Contents of EVEN

22 44 66 88

Unit - 11

Templates and Exception handling

11.1 Introduction :

- Template is one of the features added to C++ recently. It is new concept which enables us to define generic class and function and thus provides support for generic programming. Templates supports for generic programming.
- Generic programming is an approach where generic types are used as parameters in algorithm so that they work for a variety of suitable data types and data structure.
- A template can be used to create a family of classes and functions. For example, a class template for an array class would enable us to create arrays of various data types such as int array and float array. Similarly we can define a template for a function say mul ( ), that would help us create various versions of mul ( ) for multiplying int, float and double values.
- A template can be considered as a kind of macro. When an object of a specific type is defined for actual use, the template definition for that class is substituted with the required data type. Since a template is defined with a parameter that would be replaced by a specified data type at the time of actual use of the class or function, the templates are sometimes called parameterized classes or functions.

11.2 Class Templates :

- Templates allow us to define generic classes. It is a simple process to create a generic class using a template with an anonymous type. The general format of a class template is :

```
template <class T>
class classname
{
        //      ... ...
        //      class member specification
        //      with anonymous type T
        //      wherever appropriate
        //      ... ...
};
```

Example :

```
template<class T>
class vector
{
        T* v;
        Int size;
        public :
        vector(int m)
        {
                v = new T[size = m];
                for(int I =0; I < size; i++)
                        v[i] = 0;
        }
};
```

Now in main function vector of various types can be created using following ways.

```
vector<int> v1(10);            // 10 element integer vector
vector <float> v2(25);         // 25 element float vector
```

The type T may represent a class name as well. For example

```
vector <complex> v3(5); // vector of 5 complex numbers.
```

- *A class created from a class template is called a template class. The syntax for defining an object of a template class is :*

  Class-name <type> objectname (arglist);

- *This process of creating a specific class from a class template is called instantiation.*

Function Templates.

- Like class templates, we can also define function templates that could be used to create family of functions with different argument types. The general format of a function template is :

```
Template<class T>
returntype functionname(argument of type T)
{
        //      ... ...
```

```
        //      Body of function
        //      with type T
        //      wherever appropriate
        //      … …
}
```

- The function template syntax is similar to that of the class template except that we are defining function instead of classes. We must use the template parameter T as and when necessary in the function body and in its argument list.

```
template <class T>
void swap(T& x, T& y)
{
        T temp = x;
        x = y;
        y = x;
}
```

- This essentially declares a set of overloaded functions one for each type of data. We can invoke the swap ( ) function like any ordinary function. For example, we can apply the swap() function as follows:

```
void f(int m, int n, float a, float b)
{
        swap(m, n); //swap to integer values
        swap(a, b); //swap to float values
        // ………………………..
```

This will generate a swap() function from the function template for each set of argument types.

Example :

```
#include <iostream.h>

#include <conio.h>

template <class T>

void swap(T &x,T &y)

{

        T temp=x;

        x=y;

        y=temp;

}

void fun(int m,int n,float a,float b)

{

        cout<<"\n m and n before swap:"<<m<<"  "<<n;
```

```
        swap(m,n);
        cout<<"\n m and n after swap:"<<m<<"   "<<n;
        cout<<"\n a and b before swap:"<<a<<"  "<<b;
        swap(a,b);
        cout<<"\n a and b after swap:"<<a<<"   "<<b;
}
int main()
{
        fun(100,200,11.22,33.44);
        getch();
        return 0;
}
```

- Another function often used is sort ( ) for sorting arrays of various types such as int and double.
- A function generated from a function template is called ***template function.***

Function Templates with Multiple Parameters :

- Like template classes we can use more than one generic data type in the template statement, using a comma-separated list as shown below :

```
template<class T1, class T2, … …>
return_type function_name(argument of type T1, T2, … …)
{
        … …
        … … (Body of function)
        … …
}
```

Example :

```
template<class T1, class T2>
void display (T1 x, T2 y)
{
        cout << x << " " << y << "\n";
}
int main( )
{
        display (1999, "C++");
        display (12.34, 1234);
        return 0;
}
```

Output :

```
199   C++
12.34 1234
```

Overloading of Template Functions

- A template function may be overloaded either by template functions or ordinary functions of its name. In such cases, the overloading resolution is accomplished as follows:
    1. Call an ordinary function that has an exact match.
    2. Call a template function that could be created with an exact match.
    3. Try normal overloading resolution to ordinary functions and call the one that matches.
    4. An error is generated if no match is found.
    5. No automatic conversions are applied.

Example :

```
template<class T>
void display (T x)
{
    cout << "Template Display " << x << "\n";
}
void display (int x)
{
    cout << "Explicit  Display " << x << "\n";
}


int main ( )
{
    display (100);
    display (12.34);
    display('C');
        return 0;
}
```

Output :

```
Explicit display: 100
Template display: 12.34
Template Display: C
```

Member Function Template

- Member functions of the template classes themselves are parameterized by the type argument to their template classes and therefore these functions must be defined by the functions templates.

```
template<class T>
Returntype classname<T> :: functionname(arglist)
{
        … …
        … … (Body of function)
        … …
```

```
}
```

- For Example the vector class and its member functions are defined as follows

```
template<class T>
class vector
{
        T* v;
        int size;
      public :
        vector (int m);
        vector(T* a);
        T operator * (vector & y);
};
template<class T>
vector<T> :: vector (int m)
{
        v = new T[size = m];
        for (int I =0; I < size; i++)
                v[i] = 0;
}

template<class T>
vector<T> :: vector (T * a)
{
        for (int i =0; i < size; i++)
                v[i] = a[i];
}
template<class T>
T vector<T> :: operator* (vector & y)
{
        T sum = 0;
        for (int i =0; i < size; i++)
                sum += this -> v[i] * y.v[i];
        return sum;
}
```

Non Type Template arguments

- It is possible to use non-type arguments, that is, in addition to the type argument T, we can also use other arguments such as strings, function name, constant expressions and built in types. Consider the following example.

```
template<class T, int size>
class array
{
        T a[size];            //automatic array initialization
        // … …
```

```
        // … …
    };
```

- This template supplies the size of the array as an argument. This implies that the size of the array is known to the compiler at the compile time. The argument must be specified whenever a template class is create.

```
    array<int, 10> a1;          // array of 10 integers.
    array<float, 5>             // array of 5 floats.
    array<char, 20>             // string of size 20
```

- The size is given as an argument to the template class.

Exception Handling

- We know that it is very rare that a program works correctly first time. It might have bugs. The two most types of bugs are logic errors and syntactic errors. The logic errors occur due to the poor understanding of the problem and solution procedure. The syntactic errors arise due to poor understanding of the language itself. We can detect these errors by using exhaustive debugging and testing procedures.
- We often come across some particular problems other than logic or syntax errors. They are known as exception.
- Exceptions are run time anomalies or unusual condition that a program may encounter while executing.
- Anomalies might include conditions such as division by zero, access to run an array outside of its bounds, or running out of memory or disk space.
- ANCI C++ provide built-in language features to detect and handle exceptions which are basically run time errors.

Basic of Exception Handling :

- The purpose of the exception handling mechanism is to provide means to detect and report an "exceptional circumstance" so that appropriate action can be taken. The mechanism suggests a separate error handling code that performs the following tasks.
    (1) Find the problem (Hit the exception)
    (2) Inform that an error has occurred (Throw the exception)
    (3) Receive the error information (Catch the exception)
    (4) Take the corrective action.(Handle the exception)
- The error handling code basically consists of two segments, one to detect errors and to throw exceptions, and the other to catch the exceptions and to take appropriate actions.

Exception Handling Mechanism:

- C++ exception handling mechanism is basically built upon three keywords :
    1) try
    2) throw
    3) catch

- The keywords try is used to preface a block of statements (surrounded by braces) which may generate exceptions. This block of statements is known as try block.
- When an exception is detected, it is known using a throw statement in the try block.
- A catch block, defined by the keywords catch 'catches' the exception 'thrown' by the throw statement in the try block, and handles it appropriately. The relationship is shown in Figure.

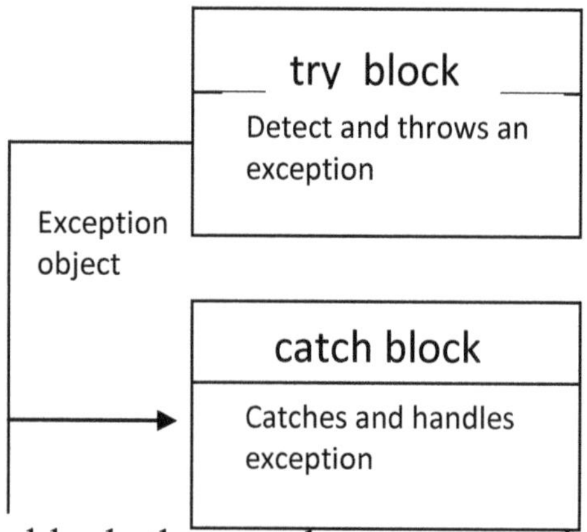

- The catch block that catches an exception must immediately follow the try block that throws the exception. The general form of these two blocks are as follows:

```
................
try
{
        ............
        throw exception;  // Block of statements which
        ............      // detects and throws an exception
        ............
}
catch (type arg)
{
        ............      // Block of statements that
        ............      // handle the exception
}
..............
```

Example :

```
#include<iostream.h>
int main( )
{
        int a, b;
        cout << "Enter values of a and b :";
```

```
        cin >> a >> b;
        int x = a – b;
        try
        {
                if (x != 0)
                {
                        cout <<"Result(a/x) = " << a / x << "\n";
                }
                else
                {
                        throw(x);
                }
                catch(int i);
                {
                        cout << "Exception caught  : x = " << x << "\n";
                }
        cout << "END \n"
        return 0;
}
```

Multi Catch Block Statement Example:

```
#include<iostream.h>
void test(int x)
{
        try
        {
                if(x == 1)
                        throw x;                // int
                else  if(x == 0)
                         throw 'x';             // char
                else if(x == -1)
                        throw 1.0;              // double
                cout << "End of try-block \n";
        }
        catch(char c)                           // Catch1
        {
                cout << "Caught a character \n"
        }
        catch(int m)                    // Catch 2
        {
                cout << "Caught an integer \n"
        }
        catch(double d)                 // Catch 3
        {
                cout << "Caught a double \n";
        }
```

```
cout << "End of try-catch system \n\n
}
int main()
{
        cout << "Testing Multiple Catches \n"
        cout << x == 1 \n";
        test(1);
        cout << "x == c \n";
        test('c');
        cout << "x <= -1 \n";
        test(-1);
        cout << "x == 2 \n";
        test(2);
        return 0;
}
```

The output of the Program :

```
Testing Multiple Catches
x==1
Caught an integer
End of try-catch system
x == O
Caught a character
End of try-catch system
x== -1
Caught a double
End of try-catch system
x == 2
End of try-block
End of try-catch system
```

Multiple Choice Questions

1) What is the correct value to return to the operating system upon the successful completion of a program?
   A) -1 B) 1
   C) 0 D) Programs do not return a value.
2) What is the only function all C++ programs must contain?
   A) start() B) system() **C) main()** D) program()
3) What punctuation is used to signal the beginning and end of code blocks?
   A) { } B) -> and <- C) BEGIN and END D) (and)
4) What punctuation ends most lines of C++ code?
   A). (dot) **B) ; (semi-colon)** C) : (colon) D) ' (single quote)
5) Which of the following is a correct comment?
   A) */ Comments */ B) ** Comment ** **C) /* Comment */** D) { Comment }
6) Which of the following is not a correct variable type?
   A) float **B) real** C) int D) double
7) Which of the following is the correct operator to compare two variables?
   A) := B) = C) equal D) ==
8) Which of the following is known as insertion operator?
   A) ^ B) v **C) <<** D)>>
9) Which of the following is known as extraction operator?
   A) >> B)<< C)< D)>

10) Object oriented follows __________ approach in program design.
A) Top-down **B) Bottom-up** C) Linear D) none

11) The wrapping up of data and functions into a single unit is called____________
A) Data Binding **B) Encapsulation** C) Abstraction D) None

12) In OOP, the concept of inheritance provides the idea of ______
A) Reusability B) Rewriting C) Polymorphism D) Class

13) _______ means the ability to take more than one form.
A) Inheritance B) Data hiding C) Data abstraction **D) Polymorphism**

14) Dynamic binding is also known as ___
A) Early binding B) Static binding **C) Late binding** D) None

15) C++ was developed by _______
A) Bjarne Stroustrup B) Denish Ritchie
C) Berners-Lee D) None

16) The multiple use of << in one statement is called _______
A) Polymorphism B) Inheritance C) Reusability **D) Cascading**

17) In C++, a function contained within a class is called _________
A) Non-member function **B) Member function**
C)Static function D) None

18) The concept of using one operator for different purpose is known as ________
A) Operator overloading B) Operator overriding
C) Function overloading D) none

19) _________ provides an alias for a previously defined variable.
A) Variable B) **Reference variable**
C) Pointer variable D) none

20) The standard C++ comment
A) / **B) //** C) /* and */ D) None of these

21) C++ provides a qualifier called ______ to declare named constants.
A) Const B) Default C) cast D)None of these

22) A const modifier defaults to ______.
A) Float **B) int** C) char D) double

23) ___________ Variable must be initialized at the time of declaration.
A) Pointer B) Local C) Global **D) Reference**

24) In C++ the main() returns a value of type int to the _____
A) Compiler B) Interpreter
C) Operating System D) Function

25) ________ gives the compiler the details about the functions such as the number and types of arguments and type of return values.
A) Function Definition **B) Function Prototyping**
C) Main() D) None

26) When a function is declared _________ the compiler replaces the function call with the respective function code.
A) Static B) Const **C) inline** D) private

27) The member functions defined inside the class are by default treated as_____
A) Static B) Const **C) inline** D) private

28) An argument to a function can be declared as ______, indicating that the function should not modify the argument.
A) Static **B) Const** C) inline D)private

29) _______ is a way to bind the data and its associated functions together.
A) Structure B) Union **C) Class** D) None of these

30) The keywords private and public are known as __________.
A) Visibility labels B) Mode C) class members D) functions

31) Visibility labels are followed by a _____.
A) Dot (.) B) Semicolon (;) **C) Colon(:)** D) Comma (,)

32) The variables declared inside the class are known as _______.
A) Data members B) Member function C) Static function D) static members

33) The functions declared inside the class are known as _______.
A) Data members **B) Member function** C) Static function D) static members

34) The symbol _____ is called the scope resolution operator.
A) ;; B) # C) * **D) ::**

35) The 'class name ::' is known as _______.
A) Special member B) Member class
C) **Membership label** D) none of these

36) _________ can access the private data of the class.
A) Data members **B) Member function** C) Static function D) static members

37) A _________ can call another member function directly, without using the dot operator.
A) Data members **B) Member function** C) Static function D) static members

38) ________ is initialized to zero when the first object of its class is created. No other initialization is permitted.
A) Data members B) Member function
C) Static function **D) static data members**

39) Only one copy of ______ is created for the entire class and is shared by all the objects of that class, no matter how many objects are created.
A) Data members B) Member function
C) Static function **D) static data members**

40) ________ is visible only within the class, but its lifetime is the entire program.
A) Data members B) Member function
C) Static function **D) static data members**

41) A____ can have access to only other static members declared in the same class.
A) Data members B) Member function
C) Static member function D) static members

42) A ________ can be called using the class name.
A) Data members B) Member function
C) Static member function D) static members

43) Memory space for _________ is allocated separately for each object.
A) Functions **B) Member variables**
C) Member functions D) None of these

44) Memory space for ________ is allocated only once and shared by all objects.
A) Variables **B) Member functions**
C) Data members D) Constant

45) __________ function has access to the private members of the class.
A) Friend B) Static C) Const D) none of these

46) If a member function has ______ argument, then we cannot alter the data in the function.

A) Friend **B) Const** C) Static D) Extern

47) ________ is a special member function whose task is to initialize the object of its class.

A) Destructor B) friend function **C) Constructor** D) None of these

48) Constructor cannot have ___________, not even void.

A) Data type **B) Return type** C) static data D) Const data

49) Constructors should be declared in _________ section.

A) Private B) Protected **C) Public** D)Safe

50) ________ has the same name as that of a class.

A) Friend function B) Destructor C) Static function **D) Constructor**

51) A ______ is used to destroy the objects that have been created by the constructor.

A) Destructor B) Constructor C) Constant function D) Destroyer

52) The destructor is a member function whose name is the same as the class name but is preceded by a ______.

A) : (colon) B) **~(tilde)** C) ; (semicolon) D) none of these

53) The keywords private and public are known as __________.

A) Access Specifier B) Mode C) class members D) functions

www.ingramcontent.com/pod-product-compliance
Ingram Content Group UK Ltd.
Pitfield, Milton Keynes, MK11 3LW, UK
UKHW061507190726
13845UKWH00029B/1026

9 789384 644338